CW01471752

0

Acknowledgements

I wish to thank Martyn Boyd of NorthLight PhotoArt for allowing me to use his superb photograph of the Spirit of Great Britain Vulcan on the cover of this book. Martyn can be reached at: northlightphotoart@icloud.com.

I also want to thank Simon Ham for his sterling work in proof reading this book; suggesting better technical explanations; correcting my syntax, grammar, typos and my punctuation too.

I want to mention also the Newark Air Museum, a jewel of a museum where Lancasters, Spitfires and Hurricanes only take up a small corner of one of the hangars. The museum houses a Vulcan and a host of Cold War aircraft. The staff and volunteers have been helpful in sharing memories and stories, some of which appear in this book.

I'd like to thank the Professional Pilots Rumour Network (PpruNe) for the story in Chapter 11, of the *No.1 Group Dining-In* event at RAF Waddington in the mid-60s. It expanded my own knowledge of that fun night!

Lastly, I'm grateful to KDP, the self-publishing facilities run by Amazon. The idea of publishing this book, and my previous one, would never have entered my mind had it not been for KDP. It has been quite an adventure to go through all the hoops required for self-publishing, but well worth it.

To Carole, my wife and partner of nearly 60 years, who will never be a second violin to a Vulcan:

And to our daughter Michelle, who remains cheerful and funny in spite of her long illness.

Twenty Years Flying Vulcans

Introduction

My years on the Vulcan aircraft started in February 1962 and ended in June 1982 when I lost my medical category preventing me from flying at all.

I started my years on the Vulcan as a co-pilot on 83 squadron, then as a captain on 617 squadron, followed by two tours as a flying instructor on 230 Operational Conversion Unit. These two tours were interrupted by a tour in Cyprus in charge of the Vulcan Training Complex (Pilot flight simulator, navigation and bombing system simulator and air electronics simulator). My final four years were spent as a Vulcan examiner on No. 1 Group Standardisation Unit. I cannot think of any period of my time on Vulcans which was unpleasant. There were times when I was frustrated, often by my own actions, or disappointed in the way the RAF ran certain aspects of its existence.

Some may find it strange spending twenty odd years flying the same aircraft when, if I had chosen, I might have had a more varied flying life. Although that is true, my worry was that there was every chance that I might end up flying a desk. I would not have liked that. But I knew that if I concentrated on flying the Vulcan, I would be assured more than less, of continuous or near continuous flying. Training aircrew on different aircraft is expensive and the RAF looked kindly to those who chose to fly the same aircraft for long periods. There are plenty who did that. The other aspect is that had I been promoted, I would have one flying tour in the new rank then, if no further promotions came, I would be stuck on the ground.

Having chosen to fly the Vulcan, I worked hard at improving my skill and knowledge of the aircraft in its various roles. In that, I was successful. My 10 last assessments (a copy of which I obtained from the RAF through the Freedom of Information Act) all recommended promotion, but added that I did not wish to be promoted. My ground tour in Cyprus proved to me and the assessors that indeed I had very good potential for promotion. On the other hand, I knew that it was most unlikely that I be promoted further to Wing Commander. That was my problem and my fear: one flying tour in rank and that's it! I really wanted none of it.

The Vulcan was a marvellous aircraft to fly. It was powerful, manoeuvrable and more than capable of carrying out the task it was designed for. Being a member of a crew of five professional aircrew gave me a wonderful feeling. A feeling of being in a family, on which I depended and who depended on me. Over the years I flew with crews that seemed to be telepathic. They talked little yet did their job in an admirable and thorough manner. On the other hand, I flew with crews that simply did not gel. With those, the atmosphere could be unpleasant and at times could be downright dangerous.

There were some tiresome duties such as exercises called in the middle of the night or Quick Reaction Alert (QRA) on Christmas or New Year Day. But these were just part of an era in which I was very lucky to be involved. The cold war, in my opinion was a period of considerable stability between the two sides. We knew what they were doing and planning and worked to stop it happening. They knew what we were doing and planning too: Deuce. It was a time of mutually assured destruction (MAD), and that stopped leaders from going over the top. It was not uncomfortable although occasionally, one side or the other worried about the other's leadership or intellectual ability. Other than Khrushchev trying it on in Cuba in 1962 (and soon realising his mistake) our leaders, as well as the opposition were rational, fairly cool and busy doing other things, like invading Afghanistan, or Vietnam.

I started flying in 1955 and stopped in 1982. In my estimation, these were the best years to be a pilot. Real flying: accuracy; leadership; knowledge; and resourcefulness were the usual qualities of good pilots and good crew captains. There were no electronic computers that looked after the engines, the airframe and just about everything else. Responsibility for doing the job and looking after each other was ours. Throughout that period, I felt like a pilot. Things or systems did not override my actions. But I could override them. When things went wrong, we had to deal with them. If I made a mistake, the costs could be considerable.

This book covers in more details the time period of which I have written in my autobiography, "Lucky Me! Serendipity". Some of the text has been filched directly from that first book. It saves a lot of typing. I have reviewed the text I copied and I hope there are many fewer typos, misspellings; less bad punctuation and grammatical errors. It does not mean it is perfect.

This book lays down many more of the wonderful memories I have of that long period which, as time passes (I am 83 as I write this) do not fade away.

CHAPTER 1 – Start Here

I came to the UK in September 1961 to join the Royal Air Force (RAF). I had already spent the previous six years as a trainee pilot then a flying instructor and lastly a unit test-pilot on Harvard aircraft in the Royal Canadian Air Force (RCAF).

From the early 1950s until 1960, most NATO European countries had sent a number of their trainee pilots and navigators to be trained to "wings" standard in Canada. When the scheme ended, there was a surplus of RCAF instructor pilots and navigators. They were made redundant. The RAF, wise to the idea of enrolling fully trained aircrew, trawled across Canada and caught some 50 of us.

When I presented myself at the Air Ministry in London in September 1961, I was told that I would flying Vulcan aircraft. What joy! I had only read briefly about the Vulcan in flying magazines in the officers' messes in the RCAF. This was a cutting-edge aircraft, brand new and nuclear armed!

But first, I had to convert to flying jet aircraft. I had a very few hours on the T-33, the RCAF's jet trainer, which I flew as part of my training at the Advanced Flying School in the RCAF. The conversion, which the RAF called refresher training, took place on Meteor aircraft. In spite of the "refresher" name, this was all new to me. For a start, the aircraft, old as it was, was strange to me but it performed well. Then there was the weather which took me some time to adapt to. In addition, to confuse me further, the RAF uses the proper ICAO phonetic alphabet of Alpha, Bravo…Zulu. I was used to Able,

Baker…Zebra. Then the RAF had its own way of doing things. They were quite different from the air force I'd come from, in spite of similar uniforms and rank structure. There was a lot to assimilate in addition to flying: driving on the other side of the road; (I had to take the driving test as my Canadian driver's licence was not recognised); using pounds, shillings and pence (that took some getting used to); bitter beer; very twisty roads, etc. But of course, exquisite buildings, villages, country side and lots of tradition.

Eventually it all came together and I found myself in February 1962 at RAF Finningley, near Doncaster as a co-pilot trainee in No.16 Vulcan B Mk2 course on 230 Operational Conversion Unit (OCU). I think there were 20 of us on the course to be formed into 4 crews each consisting of two pilots; the captain and the co-pilot; two navigators, the radar operator/bomb aimer, the plotter; and an air electronics officer. It was intriguing how we sorted ourselves out in crews without any help or direction from above, but mainly in the officers' mess bar.

In the late 50s and early 60s Vulcans Mk 2 and Victors Mk2 were indeed fine examples of British cutting-edge technology. These were the days of analogue electronics. Of course, there were transistors and a few printed circuits boards. But the majority of the work was done by electronic valves which generated prodigious amounts of heat and required prodigious amounts of electricity and often, cooling.

At this point I admit that it is difficult to explain how we operated the Vulcan without giving you, the reader, a little technical knowledge; not in depth but enough for you to feel comfortable with some terms that follow.

CHAPTER 2 – Technical Talk

Both the mark 2 versions of Victors and Vulcans electrical systems used alternating current which was quite unlike any of their predecessors using direct current. In the Vulcan, each engine had its own alternator producing some 32 kilowatts (Kw) of power. This was supplemented by an auxiliary power unit.[1] This APU was equipped with a 24Kw alternator. It could also generate air under pressure to start the engines, and provide cabin air conditioning. In addition, an emergency ram air turbine whose alternator produced up to 17 Kw of electricity could be released into the airflow below the port wing.

The major reason for all this electrical power was that vital parts of the aircraft, the flying controls, were powered by electrohydraulic motors whose loss of power would make the aircraft uncontrollable. Also, the navigation system itself used a fair amount of electricity. But the biggest consumer by far was the electronic countermeasures system: the radar jammers. The airbrakes (square panels which opened on the top and bottom of the wing) were electrically operated too.

The Vulcan's hydraulic system raised and lowered the undercarriage, powered the wheel brakes, nose wheel steering, the bomb bay doors as well as a few minor functions. Hydraulic pumps were fitted on numbers 1,2 and 3 engines. In addition, an electrically driven pump could provide hydraulics to the

---

[1] We called it the AAPP, or Auxiliary Airborne Power Plant. It was also known as the Rover as it was the same small jet engine that the Rover Car company had produced unsuccessfully in the 1950s to power a car

brakes but it was basically designed to open the bomb doors if the main system failed. A pneumatic system was used to close the entrance door and open it in an emergency. An additional pneumatic system eventually was installed to provide high pressure air to rapid-start the engines. Oxygen bottles for the crew were housed in the bomb bay area.

Both pilots sat on Martin Baker Mark 4 ejection seats which could be used at ground level at a minimum speed of 80 knots. The rear crew however, the two navigators and the AEO, had no such luxury. Their seats initially were only moveable fore and aft on rails. Their only exit in an airborne emergency was to slide down the entrance door. Eventually, more sophisticated seats were installed for the rear crew , where the two outer seats could swivel toward the exit, then on pulling a lever, a seat cushion inflated that pushed the occupant toward the door. The middle seat, the navigator plotter's, did not swivel and could only move fore and aft. The crew parachutes (rear crew and pilots) had self-contained oxygen bottles in case of a bailout above 10,000 feet. All parachutes would automatically open at about 10,000 feet although each was equipped with a manual opening handle, the rip cord.

Jet engines are fundamentally much simpler than reciprocating engines. The air is compressed at the front, then passes into the combustion chamber where fuel is injected and burned thereby increasing the gas pressure and velocity as it expands from burning the fuel. This high-pressure gas passes through a turbine then ejected at the rear through the jet pipe. The compressor at the front is driven by the turbine at the exhaust end. The higher the compression ratio the more efficient the engine is because more energy can be extracted from the fuel. There are two types of engine compressors set at the front of the unit: centrifugal, and axial flow. The centrifugal flow compressor flings air to its outer casing compressing through centrifugal force. The axial flow passes air through a series of fan-like blades through an opening of decreasing diameter, thereby increasing the compression ratio.

The axial flow engines fitted to the Vulcan were called Olympus. They were made by Bristol Engines in the early 50s and were of novel design.[2] As with all axial flow compressors, air was passed through a row of rotating blades in a narrowing opening, driven by the turbine at the exhaust of the combustion chambers. The difference with the Olympus engine was that there was a second compressor running independently behind the first effectively multiplying the output of the first unit. This was one of the first jet engine to use twin compressors, or twin-spool arrangement. Indeed, it was the first of its type in the world to come into service. Using this method, for example, a compression ratio of about 9 to 1 (3:1 on the first spool, and the same through the second one.ie 3x3) could be achieved. If it had been a single compressor, the ratio would have been only 6 to 1. [3]

---

[2] The Bristol Engine company was absorbed by Rolls-Royce in the 1960s.

[3] Many modern jet engines often use 3 compressors, the first one frequently a very large fan which, like a shrouded propeller, pushes a considerable proportion of its output straight out of the back, by-passing the combustion chambers and turbines. The 3-spool engine achieves compression ratios of 40:1 or more, which extracts much energy from the fuel, making it four times more economical that the Vulcan engine. Supersonic aircraft cannot use by-pass jet engines.

CHAPTER 3 – Number 230 Operational Conversion Unit

On 230 OCU, I started a ground school period of some 8 weeks. It began with a visit to see a Vulcan close up in one of the hangars.   What an impressive machine!   I had never seen anything so imposing and at the same time sleek and menacing. Its sheer mass made me swallow a few times. I was immediately fascinated by it, yet somewhat apprehensive.   This was an aircraft and a half. I could not wait to get my hands on it.

I wondered how I would manage the course. I had never had so much to learn, most of which I had no experience to fall back on. It really was new. For example, like all military pilots at the time, I was familiar with flight instruments (those that allow flying in clouds) but the Vulcan was equipped with integrated instruments, the Military Flight System (MFS).   MFS had the compass and the artificial horizon working together. In addition, heading direction signals could be controlled by the bomb aimer during bombing runs.   Instrument Landing system (ILS) could also be incorporated in the display. Maintaining an altitude was easy and without ever looking at the altimeter (not that we neglected it).   The same with maintaining a heading or accurately turning onto a heading (true or magnetic, the choice was ours) without having to watch the compass. Wonderful stuff. The integration went as far as telling the pilot the bank and attitude required to complete an instrument approach. There were a few traps however and setting and keeping the system updated was important.   I passed many a lesson completely fascinated by this wonderful system.

The winter of 1961/62 was about average for this country. But it was my first one here. I was surprised how cold houses were and how inadequate the central heating in the Officers' Mess bedrooms when it got a little cold. I had been used to -30C and colder in western Canadian winters. Here it hardly got below zero albeit very humid. After what I thought was the fall of a small amount of snow, some 4 to 6 inches, a message on the station PA system on a Saturday morning stated: "All available personnel to report to the threshold of runway 21 for snow clearing". I could not understand the meaning, so I asked a colleague what this was about. "Exactly what it said" he responded. "We have to assist with snow clearing because the airfield is home to nuclear bombers which must be able to take off at any time". I was unsure what I could do to help. Out of curiosity I went to the threshold of runway 21 to find maybe 100 people of all ranks with shovels taking the snow from the centre of the runway, carrying it to the edges. I could hardly believe my eyes. The runway is 9,000 feet long and 200 feet wide, the equivalent of over 13 miles of normal roadway. I walked away. There was no way I was going to get involved in this. I could not believe that the RAF with cutting edge nuclear bombers, could be so ill equipped to deal with a little snow. Eventually, the service bought proper snow-clearing equipment. But not before some very amusing attempts at using home-built snow clearing kit took place.[4]

---

[4] Out-of-service Meteor engine, the Goblin, had their exhaust pipes lengthened and flattened so to blow snow and ice off the runway. It was

****

Ground school went on until the beginning of May '62. It was interesting and the instructors were knowledgeable and sympathetic to newcomers like me. There were exams at the end which, fortunately, did not dig too deeply into systems, nor in normal and emergency procedures.

In the meantime, my parents in Montreal told me that the Mounties had come round to make enquiries about me not only from them, but from some of my friend and some neighbours too. This was Positive Vetting. After all I was to be privy to the UK's atomic secrets as well as some of NATO's and SACEUR's targets in the Soviet Union and Warsaw Pact countries. I had to have a clean slate and no untoward tendencies, whatever that meant. I passed although I accidentally let information about the name of an exercise that was about to take place to someone who reported me to RAF security. I had no idea that the name, exercise Matador, was confidential as everyone was talking about it on base. I was let off with a warning.[5]

Before the simulator phase started in early May, we had to learn to survive a bail out over the sea. Off we went to

---

established that jet engines could only be operated by pilots! The engines were pulled behind a tractor. Of course, no captain would wish to be seen dead running such a contraption. Co-pilots were therefore detailed for runway snow clearance. The first time the system was used at Scampton, with these young pilots in charge, the tar joints between concrete blocks forming the runway were melted on purpose. Subsequently, airmen, qualified jet engine fitters, would do the snow and ice clearing.
[5] Kim Philby got away with a lot more.

Plymouth to be chucked into the cold waters of the English Channel, wearing only our flying suit and a life-saving jacket (may west). Each one of us was handed a dinghy pack like the one we sat on in the aircraft. Once so equipped, we were thrown off the back of an RAF rescue launch. The drill then was to pull on the cord that inflated the dinghy, climb aboard (struggle rather than climb really), empty the dinghy of the sea water which always filled it as it inflated, inflate the floor, pull the protective cape over your head then settle shivering waiting for a helicopter to find you and winch you aboard back to the launch. I thought myself lucky that one of the dinghies did not inflate as expected when the user pulled the handle. A new dinghy was thrown to the user who by then was probably freezing. That time the system worked well and the dinghy inflated. I was the last to go and the faulty dinghy had been inflated by the launch crew and handed to me. Great! I jumped off the back of the launch planning to stay dry as the dinghy hit the water. I would just need to turn round and wait for the helicopter. As soon as I hit the water I flipped over, filling the dinghy to the brim. It was a struggle then to get in. It took some time before I could empty it. In the meantime, I had drifted well away from the rest of the survival victims and the sea was getting quite rough. I could see neither the launch nor the helicopter. I thought I would have to use my emergency beacon after all until I found out that it was only a dummy unit, a block of wood of the right dimensions. Eventually, as it was getting dark, I was found and winched aboard to be returned to shore.

All this dunking was followed by a two-day course on aero medicine which included a simulated emergency depressurisation from the normal Vulcan cabin altitude of about 9,000 feet to 56,000 feet. Above about 45,000 feet, if the cabin depressurises, the oxygen breathed in cannot penetrate into the walls of the lungs for lack of pressure, even when beathing 100% oxygen. The solution is pressure breathing when O2 under pressure is pushed into the lungs, forcing it to penetrate the lung walls. A problem then arises; the lungs expand and could be damaged. The solution to that is to provide a counter-pressure on the chest by wearing a jerkin which inflates as pressure breathing begins. A new problem arises. Blood from the chest cavity is forced down into the legs. This is solved by having G-trousers (used mainly by aircrew subjected to high G forces to stop the blood draining into the legs) which inflate. Once the pressure jerkin and the G-trousers are inflated, I looked like the Michelin man, and found it a struggle to breathe out. As soon as my mouth opened pure oxygen rushed in. Pressure breathing is hard work and for that reason, if the cabin depressurises at 56,000 feet, it is imperative to descend to 40,000 feet and below within two minutes.

Having dealt with the problems of bailing out into the sea and being blown up like a balloon, the real work now started. Unlike modern simulators, the Vulcan flight simulator was firmly bolted to the floor. The flight deck reproduced accurately ejection seats, straps, connectors, instruments. It also made appropriate noises. The instructor and his assistant played the part of the crew chief helping us to strap in, then of other crew members. Although we had had a substantial pre-simulator flight briefing, there was a lot to cover particularly for me, as a complete newcomer. My captain, Colin, had already had a tour as a co-pilot on Vulcans and had been checked out in the left-hand seat, so I was the major beneficiary. What a lot to take in. Although I had used the simulated fuel control panel in ground school, the real one (well, at least in the sim) took some time to get used to. It is situated between the seats and one needed to look to see the switches and buttons. Room in the Vulcan flight deck is at a premium. Trying to read fuel tank contents just ahead of the throttle quadrant, and write them down on the fuel-check form in the plasticised pages of the A5 book held on my right knee, then add them up, transfer the information onto a howgozit graph seem to take such a long time. I really felt left behind as the rest of the pre-flight checks were carried out.

Let me define and explain the howgozit graph. The graph is a forecast of the fuel used during a sortie. On the left-hand scale, the amount of fuel in pounds, at the bottom the time. Before flight, a line is drawn on the graph showing the expected fuel at specific time. The idea is that when a fuel check is done and the time noted, the total is marked on the line on the graph and compared with the expected amount. Amounts such as fuel used to start the engines, taxy and take-off are known. That is the start point on the graph. To complete the graph reference is made to one of the many pages of graphs and tables in the Operating Data Manual which show fuel used for climb (standard or operational), and consumption at certain altitudes and airspeeds. In addition to keeping control of fuel consumption, the co-pilot also has to work out the aircraft's centre of gravity. This is done with a special slide rule which covers the weight of every piece of equipment the aircraft carries and its effect on the position of the centre of gravity (CG). Centre of gravity control is important because if it goes outside the limits, the aircraft will become less controllable. All this has to be learned and practiced so that no undue time is used to carry out the task.

So I started in the flight simulator. A thorough briefing and other preparation prior to climbing in. The simulator was more of an environment and procedures trainer than modern equivalent. Being bolted to the ground there was no movement. Second, there were no external references; the windscreens were clear glass within a lightbox where night flying could be simulated. All the instruments, dials, switches, levers, knobs and indicators were like the real aircraft. Everything moved correctly and the machine reacted to pilot or instructor inputs (simulating emergencies) correctly. Even the noise was right. But without movement or external references, it was chiefly used to practice using the instruments (particularly the MFS) correctly, and dealing with emergencies. In that sense, the twelve three-hour exercises were extremely valuable to me as this was all very new and most impressive. I could not wait to get airborne in the real aircraft. Although control of the fuel system was not difficult, it took some getting used to. With 14 tanks to deal with and as mentioned above controlling the CG, the co-pilot, at times had plenty to do. There was some help integral to the system though. For example, control of the CG was done by a small magic-like gubbins worked by an electric motor driving a shaft on which there were 14 cams of different shapes. As the shaft turned, each cam turned on or off the fuel pump of the tank associated with it. In fact, when the whole system was active, its first action was to put all fuel pumps to half speed except the one whose cam was live. That pump ran at full speed for the time which depended on its total contents, its position in the aircraft and the effect of fuel being used on the CofG. The driving motor, cams and electrical wiring was relatively simple only because so much work had been done by the designers and engineers to establish the profile of each cam.

The fuel system was divided up into four groups, one for each engine and each group sequence timer could be on or off individually. In addition, there was a large dial on the instrument panel with needles showing the approximate position of the CofG on each side of the aircraft. It was a good, reliable system easy to operate. The CofG could be controlled to a fine degree by two transfer pumps, one per side, able to feed fuel from number 1 tank to number 7 tank, both tanks being in the same group. To achieve a specified CofG, say, for landing, fuel was normally transferred aft. The rate of flow was known so it was a matter of working out the time the pumps should be on. There has not been a single pilot in the Vulcan force who did not at one time or other (I expect many times) forget that the transfer pumps were on and when pressing the CofG dial button see both needles fly off into the red sectors. The hope, next was to have enough time to get the fuel back the other way before landing. I admit to have done that a few times, even as an examiner. And that is some admission.

CHAPTER 4 - Airborne at last.

That great event of flying a Vulcan happened on 4 May 1962 in XJ284. As we taxied out of the dispersal, I was amazed how manoeuvrable the aircraft was on the ground given its size. Nosewheel steering was precise and quick to respond. I was not used to controlling such a large aircraft, (by far the biggest I had ever set foot in). The pilots sitting so high above the ground and some 15 feet in front of the nosewheel made taxying more interesting albeit not too difficult. The brakes were very smooth, powerful and easy to use. Because of its size, I kept looking out towards the wing tips (which could hardly be seen from the flight deck). This is when my instructor simply said, "Just steer the cockpit, the rest will follow".

The take-off was breath-taking. I could hardly believe the performance of, of all things, a bomber able to climb at more than 6,000 ft per minute after take-off, and get to 40,000 feet in just a blink, it seemed to me. The instructor, Flt Lt Jones, was very good. His flying accuracy, I thought, was most impressive. I was given control during the climb. I was surprised how light and responsive the aircraft felt

Once at the top of the climb, I did my fuel check and put an "x" on the howgozit graph. Spot on the line. I did not think that these graphs were that accurate. I then worked out the CofG with the slide rule. Although this was the first time in the real aircraft, in spite of the practice in flight simulator, I was a bit slow but Jones was patient. Once I'd put my fuel book away and the slide rule, the instructor showed me how the aircraft handled and behaved under certain conditions at 40,000 ft and above. There are things that pilots read about which most have no idea what they mean and never experience. One such was the Dutch roll. I had read about it but this time, as the demonstration took place, I understood what it meant and how it happens (a combination of yawing and rolling at the same time). We accelerated to the aircraft's limiting speed of 0.93 indicated Mach number (IMN). That was by far the fastest I'd ever been. Then we did some steep turns. There again the aircraft was both manoeuvrable and stable. Steep turns at 45 degrees of bank required good concentration to maintain height and speed. What I really liked was the way the integrated flight instruments worked. No need to watch the compass, following the command indicator on the horizon instrument would simply roll out the aircraft on the selected heading. Altitude control could also be selected so that pitch control would be easy. The rest of the crew were learning too. The bomb aimer, Tony Harris was busy dropping bombs on such as Manchester and Leeds (simulated ones, of course) and the plotter, Mike Duggan, was deeply involved being amazed at all this kit under his control keeping track of the aircraft's position. Ian Hall, the Air Electronics Officer, was keeping an eye on our electrical system. He too was fascinated by all this wonderful new equipment he could play with. Eventually, after a number of fuel checks, and an attempt at CofG control, I was getting the hang of it and getting quicker too, we returned to the circuit.

Circuit work, landings and take-offs, is when a student pilot really starts sweating. The Vulcan is no exception. At first, it was not easy to manoeuvre the aircraft smoothly. I was unused to the amount of rudder required to achieve smooth and balanced turns at circuit speeds. Secondly the very nose high approach attitude was somewhat intimidating, which, together with the need to control the speed quickly and accurately, and at the end of it make a good landing was demanding. I could not get over the height at which we sat when the wheels touched the ground, and how smoothly we could return to the air applying just a fraction of the available thrust. Although all that eventually became pleasurable, it was hard work for me as a newcomer to the aircraft. (I found out later, even for experienced pilots, flying visual circuits which took only about 5 minutes of concentrated work, were very demanding and sweat making.) But too soon, our fuel was getting down to minimum (about 8,000 lbs or 1000 gallons) and we had to land. This was even more impressive. As soon as the wheels touched the ground, the nose wheel was lowered and the tail brake parachute (TBC) deployed. The deceleration was remarkable, throwing us forward into our seat harness. The use of the TBC Followed by moderate braking could stop the aircraft within 3,000 or 4,000 feet.

That was it. My introduction to the real live Vulcan. I took a deep breath, glad to have had such an experience. I could hardly express my delight after such a trip. It was unbelievable, beautiful, demanding, and pleasurable all at the same time. Quite obviously I was going to enjoy flying the Vulcan and being part of a crew. Lots and lots to look forward to.

****

At the time I was still using my RCAF flying log book and only recorded the name of the first pilot/captain and myself rather than the full crew. Also, the sorties were described too briefly leaving a big hole in what we actually did during the trip. It was not until I started on my own captaincy course in 1965 that I included the names of the whole crew and a more detailed description of what the sortie consisted of. In retrospect, I am surprised that no one on the squadron, my captain, a flight commander or even the boss, ever mentioned that I should include more details in my log book entries although someone said I should use an RAF logbook (both the RCAF and RAF pilot log books were exactly the same save for the title).

There were only two sorties with an instructor during my initial OCU course; one day sortie and the other at night. The rest of the flights were all with my own crew, with the occasional rear crew instructor using the 6th seat. The only opportunities for me to handle the aircraft in the circuit was limited to these two instructional trips. The captain, Colin Adams, was not authorised to let me land the aircraft although I remember flying most of the circuit, but he would take over in the last mile for the landing. There were 13 flying exercises on the OCU which covered just about all the basic requirements to start work on operational squadrons. There was a lot more to learn and much experience to gain once on the squadron.

CHAPTER 5 – Front Line on 83 Squadron

The Adams crew, Colin Adams, me, Tony Harris, Mike Duggan and Ian Hall arrived on number 83 Squadron at RAF Scampton, on the 27th June 1962, having been certified as proficient by 230 OCU at Finningley the day before. Except for Colin we were all single and living in the officer's mess.

Scampton has much history attached to it. The Dambusters, 617 Squadron, carried out their dams' raid from Scampton in May 1943. The squadron was still there but flying Vulcans. Scampton's runway had been lengthened to 9,000 feet. In the process the Roman road, the A15, was diverted to form a series of long curves before is regained its original path north of the airfield. The station crest was of a bow and arrow, the arrow set at an angle to the bowstring replicating the runway direction. The crest also carried the words (in Latin) "An Armed Man is not Attacked". A statement that the US gun lobbies would very much like.

The airfield has six dispersals each of which could hold four aircraft of Vulcan size, as well as the operational readiness platform at the beginning of runway 23 which also could hold four Vulcans. Each dispersal had its own technicians' huts and small workshops. Each position on the dispersal was equipped with a refuelling system so that aircraft could be refuelled directly without the use of tankers. There was a jet fuel pipeline from a major fuel depot connected to the station. This was all very sophisticated for the late 50s when the airfield was modernised. Unfortunately, the refuelling system had problems of pressure shock waves causing aircraft refuelling valves to fail. In the 20 years I knew Scampton, the system was never used.

Once I'd settled in the mess, my next ports of call were the various sections on camp where I had to present myself and sign in. The security office was probably the most important so that I could enter and leave the station at will. Then to the squadron with the rest of the crew to have a formal welcome talk by the boss, Wing Commander Ray Davenport (followed in January '63 by Wing Commander John Slessor, the son of the wartime leader Sir John Slessor). Although I was used to crew rooms, an operational front-line squadron is somewhat different. Many of us were young but we took the task of being involved in the cold war seriously.

The squadron offices were to the side of hangar number one. The four hangars could house up to 3 Vulcans for servicing and repairs. It was easy to wander in the hangar and just examine what was being serviced.[6] At the time, the squadron "owned" 8 Vulcans which were serviced by its own squadron ground crew. It was very much a joint effort to make the squadron compete and shine against the other squadrons at Scampton, numbers 617 and 27.

****

---

[6] Unfortunately, the hangar also housed Jackdaws (Hooded Crows) which nested on the high beams supporting the roof. Jackdaws liked bright items and were constantly on the lookout to steal a shiny tool or a part of an aircraft being serviced. From time to time, long extendable step ladders (called Giraffes) were used to raid the nests. Many a lost tool or a shiny pipe was recovered from those excursions.

We took some leave as a crew before starting the work of getting recategorized to combat ready. A combat-ready crew was ready for war. It meant that it would carry out Quick Reaction Alert (QRA) duties; be allocated targets in the Soviet Union; and handle all that was required when dealing with a nuclear weapon. This was a lot of responsibility, but it did not seem to weigh us down. This was our job. In any case, the captain and all of the rear crew had considerable experience of being in the front line and took to this new status as professionals. I was the only odd one in the crew that had no experience of how this all worked and what it meant.

My first flight on an 83 squadron Vulcan was on the 6th July 1962. It was an acceptance trip with our flight commander and of course my rear crew. But I had to wait until the 19th for my next sortie but this time with my crew. We took part in Exercise Kingpin and although I remember the name, I can't remember what it was about. But it was a day flight which took 4:40 hours.

During this first month, I managed to get checked out on the Chipmunk used to give air experience to RAF Air Cadets. That was good fun particularly flying from this enormous 9,000 ft by 200 ft runway, and sometimes, mixing it with the Vulcans but not very seriously.

On the 1st of August 1962 we picked up a brand-new Vulcan from its makers in Manchester. Its registration was XL392, painted in anti-flash white. Not a scratch on anything in the cabin. It had flown just 1:50 hours by Avro chief test pilot, Tony Blackman.

The Vulcan pre-flight checks the RAF used – which could last some 45 minutes – were briefly interrupted when the two of us on the flight deck saw three people dressed in white flying overalls walk in front of our aircraft and climb into another brand-new Vulcan parked alongside. The surprise was that within just a few minutes, the aircraft had its engines running and was taxing out. A couple of minutes later we heard the roar of its take-off. I subsequently found out that Tony Blackman hated wasting company time when it came to do acceptance air tests. He got the aircraft airborne as quickly and safely as possible. We, on the other hand, continued down our ponderous check list, and eventually found our way to Scampton. The flight took just 35 minutes.

We had been well treated by Avro's management. They arranged a factory visit in Chadderton, an excellent (dry) lunch in the Board's Dining Room and a return to Woodford where the Vulcans were assembled from parts which had come by road from the Chadderton factory. There was an awful lot to build and to assemble. I was fascinated both by the technology and engineering. I had read that this country, small as the UK is, could and did produce world beating aircraft and certainly be more than competitive against the big boys in the US and produce better aircraft with superior engines in the bargain. I was most impressed.

Our proficiency as a crew improved as we now started to convert to role. It was all high-level flying with simulated bombing runs on various targets which varied in difficulties. The big advantage the bombing radar had was the use of offsets. This allowed a difficult-to-find target to be attacked by using an aiming point some distance from the target where there was a good radar return, as long as the distance north-south and east-west from the target was measured accurately. Although our bombing was done from over 40,000 ft, we still took evasive action on the run in to the target. The idea was to make it difficult if not impossible for the Soviet ground-to-air missile radars to lock onto us. The attack consisted of four steep turns, the first 45 degrees from the inbound track, the next 90 degrees to cross the track then another 90 degrees turn the opposite direction and finally a 45 degree turn back on to the attack heading leaving just a few miles for final adjustments prior to bomb release. The manoeuvre demanded accurate flying and speed keeping. The ground-based Radar Bombing Scoring Unit would work out our result which was generally quite acceptable. As time went on our scores got better, but then I was never quite sure if a 500 yards error from the target would make much difference to the damage the explosion of a 1.1 megaton bomb would make.

When we became combat ready, we were allocated a target which we had to study intensely. Targets were generally military such as army camps, airfields, naval ports and sometimes police or security building in built-up areas but very few of the latter. The strategy that Bomber Command used in case of war was to use the high-level bombers (at 56,000 ft or more) on a broad front, each aircraft equipped with and using radar jammers. The idea was to cover as many frequencies as the Soviet ground and air radars used and swamp their systems. As such it made much sense judging by the experience of the RAF's Vulcans' participation in the US air defence exercises.[7] The route had to be drawn up by the navigator plotter from information about the position of defensive missile sites and airfields. However, because Gary Powers had been shot down in 1960 by a soviet missile in a U2 flying at over 70,000 ft, the change of tactics from high level to low level was being actively considered. But it would still take time before low level was implemented.

When we were programmed for a flight, we were entitled to pre-flight and a post-flight meal as well as in-flight rations. We ate in the aircrew meal centre and it was not too long before we V-bomber crews became known as part of Eating Command.   The aircrew meal centre had its own kitchen and waiting staff. Menus were varied but not that appetizing. But

---

[7] In 1960 the USAF tested its defences against incoming bombers. B52s and B47s were used to penetrate US territory. The RAF was invited to participate. Four Vulcans were sent to Bermuda from where they attacked the US east coast with full Electronic Counter Measures jammers. The whole of the east coast was blanked out – radio, TV and radar – and one undetected Vulcan flew on to land in Plattsburg, New York. Another four Vulcans attacked the US and Canada from the UK flying at 56,000 feet. One aircraft was intercepted and the other three could have bombed Washington, Chicago and New York. The USAF press release quoted a success rate in excess of 99.9%. The truth was released to the general public in 1997. The following year a similar exercise took place with much the same results. (See Wikipedia, Exercise Sky Shield 1960)

there were always a variety of pies for dessert, nearly invariably served with custard. I remember one occasion when someone asked the waiter for apple pie without custard. The waiter came back from the kitchen: "I'm sorry, sir, there is no custard". "Ah, is there any ice cream then?". "Yes sir, there is". "In that case, I'll have apple pie without ice cream".

If our flights were delayed, we often waited in the meal centre drinking coffee. The operations clerk would call us via the squawk box to advise when the aircraft was ready. I remember someone being asked how long his aircraft would be "Oh, he said, about 100 feet long". Guffaws all round. Eventually, it was realised that V-Bomber aircrew were getting heavier chomping up all that food, so the system was changed to either a pre-flight or a post-flight meal but the in-flight rations remained.

As a co-pilot on the Adams crew, I was progressing well. Our training needs were met on time and to the right standards. The nav team operated smoothly together and we all got along well. I was not a great drinker but our get together in the bar were always pleasant affairs.

We had been declared combat ready a few weeks after our arrival and were working hard to climb up the ladder of crew proficiency. One of the requirements to get up one of the proficiency steps was to get the crew's co-pilot, me, checked out in the left-hand seat, generally in preparation for a captaincy. The course was called the Intermediate Co-pilot Course (ICC) and I completed mine in November 1963. Colin had been such a good captain and teacher that I sailed through the course. Soon a captaincy would be open to me. Indeed, I had an interview with the Air Officer Commanding No 1 Group for that very purpose. "LeBrun, if you pass your promotion exams, there is a captaincy waiting for you" said AVM Paddy Dunn. I failed the exam twice but nevertheless was given a captaincy in 1965, thereby breaking the Bomber Command rule of Flight Lieutenants and above only as V-force captains.

CHAPTER 6 – Quick Reaction Alert

As a combat ready crew, we began to participate in Quick Reaction Alert (QRA) duties that each V-bomber squadron carried out. Our squadron operated a system of 24 hours on QRA every 10 to 12 days. This meant being in flying overalls at all times and ready to take off within 15 minutes - Readiness State 15 (RS15). After the hand-over from the previous QRA crew, we checked that the aircraft was ready for quick start, taxy and take-off. We also checked that the target material specific to the QRA aircraft was as per the check list. We worked on the principle of a minimum of two people in and around the aircraft at all times. There was an armed guard on permanent surveillance on the aircraft readiness concrete pan.

During the day we went to various location on the airfield: Squadron offices; rest rooms; target study secure rooms; and the aircrew restaurant. At night we slept in five-compartments caravans next to the Operations Centre. There were normally plenty of activities to keep us busy. For example, administration tasks at the squadron; sorties preparations mainly for the navigators working in conjunction with the captain's and our training requirements. These came from our six-month training schedule. We had our own crew target to study for some 6 hours a month. Our meals were taken in the aircrew restaurant in the Operations Block. We relaxed in the Operation Block, where we played bridge, watched TV or read magazines and newspapers, mostly outdated. Always in hearing of the Bomber Controller, ready to move quickly.

The Vulcan's enormous bomb bay housed a pretty big bomb when the aircraft was armed on QRA; the Yellow Sun nuclear weapon. There was a last-minute action to be performed before the weapon was made useable. It was called just that, Last-Minute-Loading (LML). This meant inserting a sphere of, I think, plutonium deep inside the warhead. The plutonium was held inside a 'gauntlet' which was pushed into an aperture on the side of the bomb. It was heavy and awkward. Our navigator radar, whose duty it was to carry out the job, was very slim and found the gauntlet extremely heavy, but somehow always managed it.

Yellow Sun nuclear bomb on its loading trolley

Exercises, called Exercise Edom, were called at any time on QRA. Although we were at readiness 15 (minutes), we still had to rush to the car and drive half way round the airfield to our aircraft. The captain carried the entrance door key. We had to identify ourselves with the armed guard as we rushed towards the aircraft. After stumbling with the door key (high up underneath the aircraft's nose, impossible to reach for our captain who was quite short unless he stood on the nose wheel chock and felt his way into the lock. This was worse at night). Once the crew was aboard, the entrance door was closed and we checked in on the radio, all the time listening to the Bomber Controller who had started all this rush by calling us to RS05 or RS02. Although we started at RS15, if it took longer than say 8 or 9 minutes from the initial alert to our checking-in, questions would be asked.

Once in our respective seat and all strapped in, we recovered our breath and listened to the controller for the next instructions. Often, this would be a reversion to readiness 15. We would then climb out, lock the door and go back to whatever we were doing. But just as often, readiness state would increase from 05 or 02. Occasionally, we would be brought up from RS15 directly to RS02. That became a bit more interesting. As soon as we got in the aircraft, the engines were started and we taxied to the holding point at the end of the runway, all the while carrying a 1.1 megaton warhead. In theory we could be scrambled from that position after confirming that the Bomber Controller's codes matched the ones we had. That would certainly indicate that the balloon had gone up. However, there was one more safety feature, at longitude 8 degrees east. If we had not received the Go Message by then, we would start a holding pattern until the go message arrived, or return to our recovery airfield. It never did of course. So we were reverted to RS15 generally but sometime we would be put back to RS05. In either case there was a long taxy back to the QRA pan and shut down.

Once back at RS15 we would vacate the aircraft, then the ground crew would do all the servicing required as though the aircraft had flown, including topping up the fuel as we used some 2,000 lbs (over 200 gallons) in our short ground borne trip round the airfield.

After all this excitement, generally crews went back to the aircrew restaurant for a coffee and a few biscuits. It was the responsibility of the captain to inform operation of our locations at all times. We had to be either near a phone or within earshot of the operations tannoy, the PA system. In the operations room a speaker connected directly to Bomber Command's control room would beep every few seconds indicating a live connection. All instructions to QRA or operations crews would come through that box. Messages always started: "Attention, attention, this is the Bomber Controller...", then an order would follow specifying both what the broadcast was about. For example, "Exercise Edom" and the readiness state. The broadcast could be directed at specific units, sometimes even crews. The message would be repeated but even before the first message was finished, crews would react, rushing to the aircraft as fast as possible.

As mentioned above, a call-out could be initiated at any time of the day or night. That is the point when the adrenaline kicked in with a vengeance. No one wanted to be the last, but someone had to be since there were at Scampton, 3 QRA crews with the armed aircraft on different dispersals. Our dispersal was on the far side of the airfield and took the longest to get to. Old Vanguard estate cars were used, driven by the crew member who got into the driver's seat first. There was always a rush for that too. There were a few tight corners on the way to the aircraft and in addition we had to cross the runway. Although we were given priority to cross, we still had to wait for the green light. On one occasion, not at Scampton, one of the bends was taken so fast that the car rolled over. Fortunately, no one was injured but the crew was late checking in on their readiness state. Another time, the driver left the car behind the aircraft where he thought it would be safe. Unfortunately, it was within the jet wash of the engine used to start the other three. To achieve this, the engine was wound up to 90% RPM. That produces a very strong blast from the jet pipe, which duly picked up the car and turned it over a few times before it came to rest.

The QRA crew cars were old and barely reliable. Indeed, on one occasion on a call out in the middle of a very cold night, one car refused to start and the crew was stranded until a crew bus was despatched and took the five frozen aircrew to the aircraft, by which time the exercise had terminated. Questions were asked. To make sure that did not happen again, battery chargers were attached to the wall at the front of the Operations Block. These were equipped with substantial quick-disconnect cables and special sockets for all three QRA cars. The cars were reversed into position and plugged in ready for rapid departures. That arrangement worked well, but of course the inevitable happened. On one occasion the cable did not disconnect and as the car departed in a hurry it pulled out the charger and part of the brick wall to which it was attached.

****

V-Force squadrons were allocated airfields to which they could disperse in the event of a political/military crisis. This was to reduce vulnerability of the force since most V-Force stations held 3 V-Bomber squadrons, some 24 aircraft. About once a year, the dispersal facilities were exercised – Exercise Kinsman - to ensure all facilities worked. The V-Bomber area on the airfield was self-supporting. All it needed from the station was air traffic control and fuel. Most crews enjoyed their detachment; a few days away from base. We undertook normal sorties from and back to the dispersal airfield. Meals were generally better than the home base Aircrew Meal Centre provided – the cook was always complimented on how well he did on such a limited choice of ingredients. We were particularly fond of triangular sausages which came in large catering-sized tins. Most of the dispersal airfields had Operational Readiness Platforms which accommodated four V-Bombers on fingers-like arrangement to one side of the runway. This allowed for very rapid starts and take-offs. At the end of the Kinsman, a scramble take off was initiated by the Bomber Controller at Bomber Command Headquarters. To see the four Vulcans taking-off within seconds of each other was very spectacular. Most of the host station personnel would be there watching the show. We returned to the home base generally satisfied with an exercise well carried out.

Vulcans in anti-flash white on an Operational Readiness Platform in the early '60s

At the beginning of the 1960s, Scampton's Operation Block housed the operations and flight planning rooms; a large briefing room; the secure vault where our top-secret target material was kept; the Station Commander and Wing Commander Flying's offices; the aircrew meal centre; and the QRA rest room. The rest/relaxation room was a bit small for three full crews but there always something to do or conversations to join. Even squadron commanders did QRA.

The boss of 617 squadron was Wing Commander George Bastard, a well-liked leader, amusing too. He was of South African origin and was very proud of his name, always ensuring that it was pronounced correctly as one would pronounce "bastard". Indeed, he told me one of his great uncles went to live in Quebec and changed his name to Le Batard. [8]

In October 1962 the world nearly came to an end: the Cuban Missile Crisis. All V-Bombers were brought to readiness, loaded with their weapons and crews, ready to go. Generating that many aircraft, weapons and crews took some time. As pointed out above, V-Force squadrons were allocated dispersal airfields to reduce their vulnerability. For this crisis we were not dispersed and stayed at Scampton. Prime Minister Macmillan very wisely chose not to disperse the V-Force which he thought could be interpreted by the Soviets as a provocative act, and enflame further an already dangerous situation. Eventually, logic as well as give-and-take by both the Soviets and the Americans calmed things down and we went back nearly to normal. Near the end of the emergency, crews were given permission to leave the station on the understanding that they would stay together in flying clothing, and be at the end of a telephone. We chose to go to the Red Lion pub in Sturton by

---

[8] We were once visited by a group of USAF senior officers. Wg Cdr Bastard was on QRA that day. One of the colonels decided to shake hands with all members of the three crews, 15 of us. As he did so, he called his name (I remember it still, Reynolds). Most of us said the usual pleasantries, "How do you do, sir? Pleased to meet you, sir", and so on. But when it came to George Bastard's turn, he replied "Bastard". The man was somewhat taken aback until he read the Wing Commander name tag.

Stow (mostly because Thelma was the bar maid). Soon after we got there, with a pint in our hands, the captain checked in to be told to return immediately. We all thought the situation had deteriorated. In fact, management realised that aircrew are not allowed alcohol 8 hours before flying. Eventually things calmed down and we went back to more or less normal duties. This episode had been quite frightening. Fortunately, it was never repeated.

CHAPTER 7 - Blue Steel

Blue Steel was introduced formally as an operational missile of Bomber Command. Three Vulcan squadrons and, I believe, as many Victor squadrons were to be equipped. Blue Steel was carried nestled underneath the aircraft connected to it via a number of clamps, cables and pipes. Both V-bombers had been extensively modified. The bomb doors were replaced with fixed concave units with small access panels. In the bomb bay itself, all sort of machinery was installed to provide hydraulic and cooling power to the missile, because the electronics produced a prodigious amount of heat. (All Blue Steel internal navigation equipment was analogue with valves and resistors, capacitors, etc.)

Vulcan Carrying a Blue Steel Missile over Niagara Falls

In order for Blue Steel to know its own position while it was attached to the aircraft, navigational information was transferred to the missile when required. Blue Steel's own inertial navigator was the size of a large coffee table. Every cubic inch of it acted as a heat source. Its accuracy was only guaranteed for ten minutes, which was its expected flight time from launch. Blue Steel's introduction included a new, updated ground position indicator (GPI Mk 6). This was quite a sophisticated piece of navigation equipment which, although chiefly mechanical, (lots of gear wheels and small electric motors) was accurate and reliable.

Before flying with Blue Steel attached to the aircraft, our crew had a comprehensive course on the missile. This dealt not only with the navigation equipment but also with the fuel it carried (high test peroxide - HTP) and more specifically, emergencies. The course was thorough and we felt quite confident that we could deal with Blue Steel in all its modes. The worst parts of the course though were the practical procedures dealing with HTP overheating and needing an emergency off-load. Special suits, face masks and gloves were donned by the navigator radar and the co-pilot. He, the co-pilot, acted as support and helper for the radar and as go between to tell the navigator plotter to activate certain valves to offload the HTP. Fitting the emergency offload pipes to the missile wearing near inflexible gloves made it very awkward. During the practice and in the real case, the aircraft engines would be kept running in case the aircraft had to be moved quickly. The noise made communications near impossible. However, eventually HTP would flow into the emergency offload pit and having proven that we could do it, we had to do it all over again to certify that we were indeed competent.

The aircraft with the missile attached did not handle any differently. A dry missile, that is one without its fuel, would weigh some 9,000 lbs, but some 15,000 lbs when loaded with HTP and kerosene and a warhead. The only action needed by the pilot in the left-hand seat, was to lower the missile's bottom fin when safely airborne, and raise it before landing. Although it was possible to land with the fin lowered, the touch down had to be very flat and no aerodynamic (nose high) braking was to be used. As far as I remember that never happened, although flight tests proved it was possible. I am not sure that the same applied to the Victor. It had a much shorter undercarriage and I seem to remember that the missile had to be jettisoned if the lower fin did not retract.

When Blue Steel was introduced, squadrons lost the ownership of their aircraft. A system of centralised maintenance was introduced and only aircrew and a few administrators were, as it were, squadron property. Our technical teams had all been swallowed into a central base. We were allocated aircraft on a random basis. Missiles were attached to aircraft on a random basis too. This meant we could not fine-tune a missile to an aircraft. When I had my own crew, this unmatching of missiles to aircraft cost us the victory during a bombing competition (see below for that story).

Whenever an exercise was called, crews, aircraft and missiles had to be generated within a certain time. After all we were all part of a war game that powers that be, tried their best to make as realistic as possible. Although crews were not generally told of the developing simulated political and military situation, some signals and messages were sneaked out for us to usually smile at. The timing of systems (crews, aircraft and missiles were a single unit) was crucial. Target times had to be met and questions asked if not. It was always more difficult to generate an aircraft and missile combination. Crews were easy to deal with. They were only human.

One clever individual, in conjunctions with the station air planners, the engineers and senior staff, had produced a very clever board. On it, each aircraft, missile, technical procedures, missile hoisting, fuelling, and lastly, making the whole system live and combat ready was covered. The board was huge and looked expensive. There were 24 Vulcans and I assume 24 missiles and warheads at Scampton. The "generating board" had every airframe on its left axis with space to add missile and crew. Time was on the bottom axis. A cursor mounted vertically moved along the base. If a system was generated on time, a switch was moved manually to light up a green light. However, if the system was late, the cursor, in passing, would switch on a red light. It was all very impressive and had been tried and tested time and again in a pretend situation.

An exercise was called and the wonderful new board was put in motion. Everyone in Operations was impressed by the way the board operated. What was important was the ability to forecast times at which systems would be live. The only snag is that the cursor ran at twice the clock rate. Everything was running late, lots of red lights. Obviously, the station was not performing well until someone pointed out, after some time, that the cursor moved at twice the normal speed. There had been some repairs and updates done to the board since it was last tried and someone mistakenly had altered the gearing from the motor to the cursor making it run a twice the correct speed. Good old analogue world. To my knowledge, the board was not used again.

CHAPTER 8 – Day-to-day and More

Other than long navigations trips and simulated bombing runs we also did some fighter affiliation at and above 40,000 ft. The Vulcan could turn inside most fighters so it was fun to let Lightings have a go at us. The Lighting was fast but had so little fuel that we could play for just a few minutes before the pilot declared "Bingo fuel" meaning, "I'm on minimum fuel and I've got to get back to base". The Javelin occasionally mixed it with us but it too could not follow our tight turn or catch us if we accelerated to 0.9 Mach or more. There were only two fighters we could not shake off, try as we did, the Sea Vixen and the Scimitar.

Once the excitement over, a normal return to base started by a long, 100 nautical miles descent, into the circuit. Circuit work was fun for the pilots but could be quite boring for the rear crew, unless they were involved. Our instrument approaches consisted mainly of ground control (GCA/PAR) or instrument landing system (ILS).

I was surprised that the ILS on certain military airfields in the UK was offset by about two degrees from the runway heading. The integrated flight instruments really came into their own when doing instrument approaches particularly in poor weather and although two degrees does not appear much, when flying an approach and the runway appears as the minimums (cloud base and visibility) is reached, that two-degree turn seems enormous and demanding. It is even worse when the cross-wind adds to the offset. Still, the main advantage of the MFS is that the pilot only needed to concentrate on the attitude indicator (bank and pitch) and the airspeed. No need to check the ILS instrument (there wasn't one) or compass, as long as the non-flying pilot set up the instrument correctly, it was all taken care of. Other than ILS and GCA/PAR, we also did internal aids approaches using chiefly the navigator radar's equipment. This was quite accurate and a good operator could get the aircraft safely to within one mile and 300 feet above ground.

After doing a few instrument circuits, each of which could take some 10 minutes to complete, we would do a few visual circuits. This required a great deal of concentration. From take-off to landing would take no more than 4 or 5 minutes, during which a lot happened. When turning right after take-off (right hand circuit), the pilot in the left-hand seat, if he was flying the aircraft could not see the runway and had to rely on the co-pilot for positioning. This required some judgment and practice. A descending turn onto final approach completed the difficult part of the circuit. It was expected that the turn would be completed and the aircraft pointing at the runway with the appropriate selection of airbrakes, at the correct speed for the last mile to mile and a half of the approach at some 500 to 300 feet above ground. A cross wind would make life particularly difficult and many a circuit was discontinued when it became obvious that the aircraft would not reach the runway.

The Scampton runway was orientated north-east south-west. We flew right-hand circuits, when the wind favoured the south-westerly runway (runway 23), because of its proximity to RAF Waddington just south of Lincoln, and left-hand circuits (runway 05) with a north-easterly wind. The prevailing wind was from the south and west which gave the pilot in the right-hand responsibility to inform the pilot in the left-hand seat that he was parallel (or otherwise) to the runway and at the correct distance then when to start the turn onto final approach. On operational squadrons, most of the time, co-pilots occupied the RHS and many a circuit was ruined from dodgy information from the co-pilot. Fortunately, I was experienced enough, having flown thousands of circuits in the RCAF and quite a few in the RAF by then, that it took me little time to adjust to the Vulcan's performance and give the other pilot accurate information. When eventually I was allowed to fly visual circuits, I found them demanding but very rewarding. Controlling the speed during a curved final approach was very important. The drag characteristics of the Vulcan are such that reacting slowly to a loss of just a few knots on the approach, could result in next few knots reducing even more rapidly. This was the making of embarrassing and possibly dangerous situations.

****

In February 1963, we had our first overseas trip to El Adem in Libya, near the city of Tobruck. Overseas trips were termed "Rangers". There were Lone Rangers which were mainly within Europe and the Middle East; Western Rangers chiefly to USAF bases (AFB) in the USA, mainly to Offut AFB, near Omaha, Nebraska, but occasionally to Canadian bases. On our first Lone Ranger we took off on time but soon after take-off some of the navigation equipment that had played up during our pre-flight checks became unserviceable. In fact, we were left with a single item of navigation equipment, the radio compass. This indicates the bearing of a radio transmitter in relation to the aircraft. Our on-board radar had packed up as well as the radar that gave drift and ground speed. A radio compass, fortunately, was sufficient for us to navigate across France as we were following high level airways with each point equipped with a transmitter that our radio compass could use. We were at the same time under military radar surveillance.

As we left UK airspace, we were handed over to French air traffic. I had never flown over France, indeed I had never been there, so I started to listen to the radio telephony (RT) traffic between the air traffic controllers and French aircrew. I soon worked out the format for position report, so as we passed overhead Rambouillet, a mandatory reporting point, I did the report in French and of course received a response in French. I never thought that the crew would not understand a word of what I said or the French reply. Perhaps it was not a good idea after all. I reverted to English for the remainder of French airspace as well as on the return to Scampton.

The little I saw of Libya did not impress me much, but it was much warmer than Scampton. A large proportion of the country is part of the enormous Sahara, so lots of sand and nothing green to see.

Although we carried an Aircraft Servicing Chief with us, the whole crew was involved in the post-flight and pre-flight servicing. My job as co-pilot was to refuel the aircraft. As usual we needed two tankers. Once fuel started to flow, I relaxed.[9]

The tanker drivers were Libyan. I was near the tankers and I noticed the driver was leaning against a large control wheel; the fuel pressure regulator. The Vulcan refuelled at a pressure of 50 psi but when I looked at the gauge, it was creeping towards 70 psi. The driver was slowly increasing the pressure unseen by me as he was leaning against the regulating wheel. No doubt this was attempted sabotage – Libyans wanted the UK and the USA out of Libya – which I should have reported but didn't.

The weekend was quiet but warm. I went into Tobruk, a town that did not impress me much. In a way we were glad to leave on Monday morning, particularly that all the equipment in the aircraft was now serviceable and stayed that way. It is amazing what a few days of properly dry weather will do to electronic equipment used to standing in the humid climate or northern Europe.

****

I managed to get checked out on the Chipmunk aircraft again. The chipmunk was used to give Air Cadets some air experience. I did a few hours of Chippy flying in the next few months with youngsters in the back seat. Most of them enjoyed that short flight with me, although a few were not so keen on aerobatics (as a matter of fact, I'm not keen on them either).

---

[9] The fuel amount (in percentage of the total) and tank selection switches were in one of the main wheel bays, together with the refuelling point. To ensure that the aircraft did not tip on its tail, I had to be certain that numbers 1 and 2 tanks of each group started refuelling first. A co-pilot did tip a Vulcan on its tail once. Not me.

On February 1st 1963 I was awarded a Green Instrument rating[10] (White, Green and Master Green rating). This was unusual for a co-pilot as most had insufficient experience. A green rating allows a pilot to fly down to a lower cloud base and poorer visibility. However, the sortie was somewhat eventful. I sat in the right-hand seat, I did the take-off, climb and level off at some 40,000 ft. At that point I noticed number 3 engine's oil pressure drop to zero. I immediately pointed that out to the captain (who was a very experienced pilot and an Instrument Rating Examiner) as I started to throttle back the engine with a view to shutting it down. The captain took over from me, and rather than shut the engine down, he asked the AEO if the 28 volts system was OK (quite a few of the engine instruments used 28 volts). Yes, was the reply at which point the captain opened the engine to maximum RPM. There was a loud crump and the RPM fell immediately to zero. The engine had blown up, but everything else was running perfectly well. The captain decided to continue my instrument rating sortie and return to Scampton to do a few circuits on 3 engines with overshoots only. I was doing most of the flying, dealing more than adequately with the asymmetric condition we were in. After the final landing and shutting down, the crew chief got an access ladder to the port engine intakes. He called us up to view the damage which had been done. Number 3 engine's blades of both stages'

---

[10] The RAF, like the RCAF, used a colour code system for pilot's certification for flying in controlled airspace and cloud as well as fly down to certain cloud base and visibility limits. WHITE was for a first-timer on the aircraft, GREEN for a more experienced pilot, and MASTER-GREEN which is self-explanatory. There were other categories for those who did the testing. Instrument Rating Examiner (IRE) and Command IRE. That last one was top of the tree.

compressors had been ripped out. Some of them had been thrown forward into the intake of number 4 engine, which looked in much the same state as number 3, but had kept running throughout. I thought this was an appalling act of airmanship by an experienced captain, and a lesson to me how not to handle an engine failure in the Vulcan.

****

In June of 1963 We had our first Western Ranger to Offutt AFB. The trip was uneventful some of it quite boring as we transited to Goose Bay in the Labrador at some 43,000 ft. Crossing the Atlantic can be interesting if one can see the Greenland ice cap. During one crossing, I could see the ice caps right to the northern horizon. In the southern part of the cap there were a few bumps (the tip of mountains) but further north, the cap became very smooth. I asked our plotter is he could work out how far the horizon was at our cruising altitude. He worked it out at over 400 nautical miles.

The transit to Offutt was a bit more exciting as we covered Quebec, lots of northern states of the USA. We also did a few simulated bomb-runs on the way there and back. Civilian traffic flew some 10,000 feet below us and many a curious pilot asked air traffic controllers to identify the aircraft "way above us". Since Offutt was frequently used as a staging post by the RAF, there was a small detachment able to deal with us very satisfactorily. We were housed in the Officers' Single quarters. We hired a car and saw a bit of Omaha and the surrounding countryside. The whole trip was not exciting. For me it was seeing things slightly more closely than I had done when I travelled in and through the US in the late 50s and early 60s. Omaha was not a big city but its shopping malls were enormous. We could also shop in the air base's BX (a more-or-less tax-free shop on military bases). Our aircraft was fitted with a large panier in which we carried a few spares leaving lots of free space. I think I bought a few glasses and some bedding. I was not flush and since I was to marry Carole at the end of the following month, buying stuff for the house seemed to make more sense. Our return journey was also uneventful. One thing I noticed is that the RCAF in-flight meals from Goose Bay were much more generous than those the RAF provided.

CHAPTER 9 – Low Level

During 1964 we started flying at low level. Low level was introduced because aircraft would remain below enemy ground-based radar and make it difficult for radars in fighter aircraft to see us in the ground clutter their radar would pick-up. Low flying can be hard on aircraft fatigue, so we were limited to a maximum surface wind of 25 knots (turbulence caused by surface wind can affect at least 2,000 ft of the lower atmosphere). We flew normally about 500 feet above ground level at about 250 knots, although we accelerated to 350 knots during the simulated attacks. Once we became more experienced, we were cleared down to 300 feet above ground.

Although we were meant to carry Blue Steel which could be launched as low as 500 feet above ground, we carried out some pop-up attacks where the aircraft climbed steeply to 11,000 feet, pushed over to level flight for the last very few miles before the target. This was in case Blue Steel was malfunctioning and unlikely to reach its target on its own. It was therefore dropped like a ballistic weapon carried in the bomb bay. This was not an easy manoeuvre to do accurately, particularly that a steady speed must be maintained at the top of the short climb. Handling the throttles was the co-pilot's job and it required a lot of concentration.

Low flying was fun especially for the pilots. But every member of the crew was busy. The navigator radar's equipment, the H2S, was useful in advising pilots of approaching obstacles; cut-offs (hill tops). The nav radar's voice would increase in pitch and volume as cut-offs got nearer. (His radar could not see beyond it). As we climbed a few hundred feet mostly gently, the radar cut-offs would fill and the next one would appear. The navigator plotter was also very busy keeping the aircraft on track from information the radar operator supplied. During those "fix" periods, radar cut-offs were unavailable so a good lookout was necessary. The AEO had to contact a number of ground stations; the low-level routes controllers; and active airfields as the aircraft passed close to flying units to warn them of our presence.

The official route covered Great Britain, starting near the Isle of Wight then clockwise across the Lizard Peninsula, West Wales, Liverpool Bay into southwest Scotland, crossing over to east Scotland over the mountains down the east coast, across the Firth of Forth, into North East England and ending up at the Wash. The route was one way, clockwise, five nautical miles wide and tightly controlled. It crossed a number of low flying zones, the activity of which we were advised by the controlling authorities. All of the route was pleasant to fly and not difficult. Some parts were spectacular in Wales and Scotland. In the early 60's Liverpool Bay always had a large number of ships waiting to be called in to the docks. We also flew special low-level routes to test our ECM equipment. One route in particular in Scotland had special attraction. The initial part was over the sea heading straight for the mountains on the Isle of Mull. We avoided them by turning right by some 60 degrees staying over the sea. At the speed we were flying, the angle of bank required to stay on the route was exactly the same angle as the slope of the hills and they followed the same curve northwards. It was such a pleasure to fly that leg and always a bit of a surprise as the painted houses of Tobermory would appear just to the left of the nose.

The Vulcan was inherently a strong aircraft. Each wings' two main spars, along the leading and trailing edges were attached to the centre section of the aircraft, forming triangles. The whole aircraft was one big triangle. Although we were limited to 2Gs, the aircraft was able to sustain at least 3Gs possibly more without damage. This inherent strength paid off, allowing the aircraft to fly at low level with a very long fatigue life. The Victor in comparison, being of a more conventional planform, did not take well to low flying. However, it turned into a magnificent airborne fuel tanker. Over time Vulcans were modified to strengthen them further, maintaining its low-level capability throughout its service life.

****

On the 27th July 1963 I married Carole at the same church her parents had married on the outskirts of Doncaster. My family, all in Canada, could not attend the wedding. My side of the aisle only held my crew with Mike Duggan, the navigator plotter, as my best man. We were all wearing our RAF number 1 uniform and all looked immaculate. It all passed very well on a superb end of July day. The following reception at Wilsick Hall extended well into the evening but the newly married couple disappeared for their honeymoon to Lake Como in Italy, on a maximum of £50 each which could be taken out of the country, travelling there in a very noisy mini-van.

L to R, Tony Harris, Carole's sister Sue, Mike Duggan, Colin Adams, Ian Hall, me, Carole, Carole's mother and sister Elizabeth

****

Because of the timing of promotion examinations (which I failed) I could not go with my own crew to take a Blue Steel to Australia for testing.[11] Altogether there were some 70 Blue Steel

---

[11] Blue Steel fuels consisted of HTP and kerosene. HTP was passed through a metal screen when it separated into very high temperature steam (600C) and O2, after which kerosene was injected and ignited providing the thrust. On one occasion the kerosene pump failed but the missile covered some 40 miles on steam alone.

missiles tested on the Australian Woomera range, near Adelaide. On June 26 1964 together with a different crew, I departed to Australia, taking a Blue Steel strapped to us: a Blue Ranger! I was not very happy of making such a long trip not with my own crew. In fact, I never really got on with the crew for a number of reasons, none of which had anything to do with my flying ability. The most memorable moments were in Gan, the southernmost island of the Maldives archipelago at 44 minutes south of the Equator. We had an alternator failure on the way from Khomaskar, in Aden and had to wait three days for a replacement. This was an opportunity to swim in warm water covering a reef which was full of most beautiful tropical fishes. On the return journey we only stopped overnight in Gan, all aircraft systems were running well. We were back in the UK on 21st of July, in time to celebrate our first wedding anniversary.

During my period as a co-pilot, the Vulcan's autopilot had not been released to service. Up to that point, all our flying was done manually. At high level we, the pilots, swapped every half hour or so. Flying accuracy became an acquired skill which was needed particularly during Astro navigation. Star shots lasted one minute and any speed or attitude deviations, even small ones, affected the accuracy of the shot. This was because the navigator radar, whose job it was to man the sextant, would find it awkward if not very difficult to keep the subject target in the sextant's sight. The procedure lasted some 10 minutes with one minute rest between each shot. When eventually the autopilot became available, the only enemy left was clear air turbulence. Until that time, the pilots could always blame clear air turbulence for their inadequate performance (not generally believed by the rest of the crew).

In addition to the autopilot, the Vulcan was chosen as a test bed for automatic landing. Airfields involved in the experiment had cables, called Leader Cables installed in a shallow trench from the end of the runway extending 3000 feet along the approach. In the aircraft, the auto-land equipment consisted of automatic throttles, leader cable receivers and an accurate radio altimeter. A modified autopilot was the main driver of the system, speed control was by auto-throttles (think of speed regulators in modern cars). The development work had been carried out at the factory by Avro's chief test pilot, Tony Blackman. The unit which was involved in the development of automatic landing was by the Blind Landing Experimental Unit (BLEU). The aircraft they used was a twin-engine propeller driven Varsity. Internal combustion engines which powered the Varsity were quick to respond to throttle movement, unlike jet engines. When automatic throttles were installed in the Vulcan it became apparent that engine response was much too slow as the speed decreased below the set value on final approach. The Vulcan drag characteristics at low speed, such as on the approach to land, were such that too much airspeed was lost before engine thrust was felt. That could cause dangerous situations to develop as well as the possibility of the system overcontrolling the speed. Tony Blackman suggested the incorporatin of a rate gyro into the system which would instantly increase (or decrease) throttle settings as the nose rose or lowered to control the speed. That did the trick. The system worked very well. However, a formal check out was required before individual pilots could carry out automatic landings. Few of us got that far. I was not chosen. But the auto-throttles could be used on their own without restrictions. The use of the auto-throttles system was nearly instinctive with on and off switches easily at hand. For that and the accurate manner the speed was maintained, Vulcan pilots must thank Tony Blackman, the Avro chief test pilot.

CHAPTER 10 - Captaincy

The end of our tour was approaching. Mike and Tony, the two navigators were posted on entirely different aircraft, Comets for Tony and another transport aircraft for Mike. Tony eventually got promoted to command a Comet squadron which carried out some rather secret things near the Soviet border. Ian also disappeared eventually to leave the service and join the Oman Air Force where he reached a quite senior rank. The captain, Colin went to learn to be a flying instructor then soon after promoted to be a flight commander at a Flying Training Station.

That left me for Bomber Command to decide. It then decided to break its own rule that only Flight Lieutenants and above could be V-Bomber captains, by giving me a captaincy. I was posted to 617 squadron after the OCU course. I was delighted. I started the course in December 1964. My crew (crews ended up picking each other more or less naturally) consisted of: co-pilot Colin A. was straight out of flying training; navigator radar/bomb aimer, Mike B., had just completed a tour on Valiants (which were then being withdrawn from service); plotter, Baz W., just back from Singapore having completed a tour on Canberras; and Tony C. the Air Electronics Officer, who also was fresh out of training. Except for the co-pilot, the rest of the crew all had specialist training before joining the V-Force: navigators on a long course at the Bomber Command Bombing School, and the AEO at a specialist electronic counter measures course. It was left to me (and the OCU) to train co-pilot, Colin. And since the OCU course only gave the co-pilot two dual/instructional sorties, a fair amount of the training and supervision was left to me.

After ground school and the 12 sorties in the pilots' flight simulator, my first dual trip took place on the 19th of February 1965 in XL824 with my instructor, John Stannard. (The RAF term for a flying instructor is QFI, qualified flying instructor). John was by far the best instructor I have ever had pleasure to be taught by. He was truly superb. When later I returned to the OCU as a QFI, we became firm friends. During my first dual flight, he soon got the measure of me and the crew. He very much left us to get on with the work at hand. I was already quite experienced both with the Vulcan and its role, having flown nearly 500 hours in the aircraft, of which over 50 hours were in the left-hand seat.

Up to the start of my captaincy course, I had been logging my time in my logbook on a single line with the name of the captain and a very brief description of the duty carried out. This was inadequate, so I started to log all the crew names and more details in the duty column. It took more space but was more indicative of what we did.

My first squadron flight was with the boss, Wing Commander Denis Heywood and his crew. This was a Kinsman exercise in an ex-USAF airfield near Liverpool. It was just a brief two-day stay and I acted as co-pilot to the boss because the squadron was shorthanded. He wanted an experienced hand to carry out this brief exercise. Just a week later, he formally checked me and my crew on 617 squadron. I think on that trip, he covered just about every failure that would affect the pilot and the handling of the aircraft. Then just a few days later, I did a night acceptance with the squadron QFI and that was me done. At least for the next few months.

****

Within just a few weeks we were combat ready. This meant QRA on a regular basis. The system was much the same except that two large wooden huts had been put up behind the operations block where we could relax, play cards and even table tennis. It took a bit longer to get to the cars in the event of a callout but the improvement was well worth it.

My tour as captain lasted until December 1967. During that time, we flew a large number of training sorties, exercises, low-level down to 300 ft at speeds up to 350knots. We carried out a large number of various types of simulated attacks, practiced simulated emergencies and got one or two real ones. Colin, my co-pilot, eventually got posted before the end of the crew's tour and replaced initially by Duncan. Co-pilots were interchangeable during a normal tour where crew constitution was important for target study and QRA, but also for everyday flight preparations and the flights themselves. Duncan had real difficulties with his hand and foot co-ordination. I've already mentioned that the Vulcan needed a boot-full of rudder at circuits speeds as turns were initiated. This was due to large deflection of flying controls to achieve a reasonable rate of roll and the one-sided drag which ensued. Consequently, after discussing the matter, he was posted to an easier aircraft to fly and replaced by Dick.

While Duncan was still my co-pilot, we took part in Bomber Command Bombing and navigation competition. Number 617 Squadron like the others at Scampton carried Blue Steel missiles (as did a number of Victor squadrons). Because the competition was split between navigation and bombing, crews were designated for one or the other of the contest. We were chosen for bombing since Mike, my bomb-aimer was by far the best Scampton could produce. We duly carried out plenty of practices but with Blue Steel, the rules were somewhat different. V-Bombers which carried ballistic bombs were judged on their own accuracy by the radar scoring ground units. Blue Steel scoring was quite different. At the simulated launch point, the position of the aircraft was marked by the scoring unit. The aircraft then followed directions provided by the missile's inertial navigator to the target which was also marked by the scoring unit. Although we tried to fly with the same missile in the run up to the competition so that we could, if possible, fine tune it, missile serviceability was such there was no guarantee that it would be available for the competition flight. That is what happened to us. Although the missile had been fine-tuned by another crew, it was not mated to our aircraft. Guarantee of its accuracy was not as assured as the missile we had groomed. The results were startling. At our simulated missile release point the position error was 30 yards. The missile's target, on the other hand was some 1000 yards in error. The winners, a Victor crew, had a missile target error of some 300 yards but their simulated missile release position error was in excess of 500 yards. Things simply cancelled out for them. I challenged the result with 1 Group but to no avail. As I said, Mike was a superb radar screen interpreter who could work things out on his screen that no one else seemed to be able to.

****

The autopilot was integrated with the MFS and the bombing radar. By selecting the appropriate options on the autopilot, the bomb aimer could turn the aircraft on whichever heading or track he wanted. We once carried a USAF aircrew officer, a Major I seem to remember, as an interested passenger for a high-level flight without carrying Blue Steel. He was particularly interested in the navigation and bombing equipment. After a while he climbed up the pilot's ladder to sneak a look outside and at our kit. Since he was on intercom, I explained to him the flight deck and pointed out the autopilot controls at the back of the fuel retractable console. I explained to him that the autopilot had an audio facility. "What do you mean?", "Well. you can tell it where to go. For example, if you were to tell it to go to Glasgow, it would turn on to a heading for Glasgow". "Really? I'd like to go to Cambridge". "OK". I said, "Go ahead and tell it to go to Cambridge". "Go to Cambridge" he said in a rather quiet voice. "No, no. You have to give it an order." I added. More loudly, he said, "GO TO CAMBRIDGE!" As soon as he said it, the aircraft started to turn in the general direction of Cambridge. He went back to the navigator's position and I heard Mike say to him "This blob on the radar screen is Cambridge, and we are pointing straight at it". Of course, all that was a sham and pre-arranged. Mike simply had to move markers to Cambridge on his radar screen and the auto-pilot did the rest. That was one impressed American. We wondered if he mentioned that to anyone else in his party and to anyone else at Scampton. If he did, they played ball with us because we heard no more from this hilarious event.

During a Goose Bay Ranger in the winter, we did some low level across the northern Canadian wilderness. We flew directly west of Goose Bay toward Hudson Bay for about 90 minutes, covering over 300 miles in a nearly straight line. It was all over snow cover forests and lakes in gently undulating hills. This was meant to represent the terrain we could fly over in the Warsaw Pact countries and the Soviet Union. We only crossed one road in all that distance and on our way back at high level, it was forests and snow-covered lakes as far as the eye could see. But I was to have a pleasant surprise in Goose Bay. A colleague and a friend, Eddy Baker (he was a Flying Officer, he too had broken through Bomber Commands Flight-Lieutenants-as-captains rule) having just arrived from the UK, told me the good news   that the RAF had decided to promote all Flying Officers with six years in rank or more (I was given four years seniority when I joined the RAF from the RCAF). This was indeed good news which meant a better salary and the status too.

****

It was not all work. I had a family and we had bought a bungalow near Lincoln for £2,950 in 1965. Carole had had a car accident on her way to work when we lived north of Scampton. She was teaching at a Lincoln school. A lorry pulled out from a side road and she crashed into it. She was in the RAF Hospital Nocton Hall for nearly a month. She had damaged her back, her neck and her left leg. In the course of her treatment, the doctors neglected to give blood thinning medicine which caused a blood clot to form in her left leg; a clot that has affected her all her life. That was in the days when seat belts were not fitted to cars and Carole was thrown around inside the car hitting various parts of her anatomy. Our new house, very close to the school employing Carole, made it easy and safe for her. I had to get used to travel through Lincoln to get to Scampton. It took longer but it was well worth it. So, with Carole teaching at a nearby school and me happy on 617 squadron we were satisfied with our lives. Salaries were not high and a monthly mortgage repayment of £11 seemed a millstone. Still, although we could afford few luxuries, our social life was very fulfilling.

During my stint on 617 squadron, I was fortunate to meet Barnes Wallis, the bouncing bomb designer. He had set up a charity after the Dams Raid to contribute to the education of children of the men of 617 squadron who had lost their lives during the raid. The charity still existed and Mr Wallis visited the squadron every other year. An official dinner was organised in his honour. On that occasion I also met Group Captain Leonard Cheshire. He had been 617's squadron commander after Guy Gibson. He witnessed the explosion of the first atomic bomb in Hiroshima from an observer B29 aircraft, which changed his life and together with his wife, Sue Ryder, set up charities.

CHAPTER 11 – Three-Counties Dining-in Night

This was the time that AOC No. 1 Group decided to celebrate the success of the V-Force, particularly the Vulcans (Number 3 Group controlled the Victors) by having a mass formal dining-in night in an arrangement of large marquees adjoining the Officers' Mess at RAF Waddington. All officers of the Groups were ordered to attend, including nurses from the RAF hospital at Nocton Hall. The numbers of people would be huge. An operation order was duly prepared and published with mandatory coach transport (although I lived just a short distance from Waddington, I still had to go to Scampton for the coach journey) from each base, Scampton, Finningley, Cottesmore and Coningsby. Each coach was planned to depart at specific times and arrive at Waddington at its allocated time.

The event did not quite go to plan. Sufficient to say that the evening was chaotic, expensive, drunken and bloody good fun, particularly in the re-telling of all the stories which emerged.

The layout of the marquees was such that only a proportion of those attending could see the top table where the brass was sitting. They were hidden and therefore free to act as they wished Pre-meal drinks (mainly sherry) were served by waiters carrying jugs of the stuff, rather than each officer picking up a dainty glass, refills and re-refills were plentiful. At the time the call was made that the meal was served, most junior officers and a few senior ones were inebriated, indeed out of control. As speech-time began (I don't even remember the Loyal Toast taking place, after which at dining-in nights, normally the mayhem began) all hell broke loose. Tucker W. a captain on 617 squadron, had an enormous Pakistani taxi horn which he blew continually every time anyone on the top table opened their mouth to start their speech. In the gents' toilets (a row of portaloos had been installed), large firework banger in the lavatory bowls wreaked havoc with some very senior officers' mess kit. And at the end of it all (the event finished early!) water from a high-pressure fire hose was sprayed over just about everyone in the senior contingent, before the hose handlers lost control of the hose, then just about everyone got a soaking. A marvellous evening was had by all of the rank of Squadron Leader and below.

I found the story of this wonderful event which appeared in PPRuNe (Professional Pilots Rumour Network) in June 2000. Already by then the tale was over 30 years old:

It was the height of the 'V' force and a misguided AOC 1 Group decided it would be an outstanding idea to have a 1 Group Dining-In Night at Waddington to which as many V force aircrew as possible would be 'invited' to attend. This function would celebrate the success of the V Force and allow the AOC to wallow in the unadulterated praise of his troops and amass bags of smartie points with the wheels from HQ Bomber Command and MOD. Given the size of the V Force in those days the numbers involved were huge and so a special working group was set up well in advance to organise the whole event and ensure everything went with 'military precision'.

As the day approached, the area surrounding the Officers Mess at Waddington was transformed by a vast series of interconnected marquees in which the dinner would be held. A vast 'Op Order' was duly dispatched to all the V Bomber units, giving everyone the fine detail of the great event. This detail even included the times for all the coaches to leave the units, ensuring they all eventually arrived at approximately the same time.

The great day dawned and the blokes, given this early example of excessive micro-management, had decided to make some alternative refreshment arrangements for the coach journeys to ensure nobody suffered from dehydration during the journey to Waddington. So, at the appointed time the coaches filled up and everyone began to get stuck into the beer crates that had been stacked on board

At 1930hrs the coaches began to arrive at Waddington with most of the occupants already 'tired and emotional' after the journey. Pre-dinner drinks only exacerbated an already volatile situation. Eventually everyone was summoned into this vast marquee, grace was said and the dinner began. From that point on things went downhill at an ever-accelerating pace. The sound system was an early victim of sabotage. The marquee itself was so vast that many of the legs could barely see the top table and, with no audible direction from on high, decided to take events into their own hands. Food was largely ignored as more and more wine, beer and spirits that had been smuggled in were consumed. Before long various altercations broke out between squadrons or individuals as old scores were settled. The stakes were soon raised as individuals began seeing who dared sabotage the most supporting elements of the marquee, interfering with the activities of some other sports enthusiasts who had begun sliding down the outside.

The top table did their best to regain control of events, but the sheer scale of the function meant that, rather like a forest fire, as soon as one element was damped down, the fire would suddenly spring up elsewhere. It was decided to curtail the event as rapidly as possible with a rousing speech from the 3*, however, the sight of him rising to his feet was the final straw and complete bedlam broke out as food and various other items flew in the direction of the top table. A general food fight ensued. It was at this point that certain individual cut the final supporting ropes on parts of the marquee. By common consent it was decided that the dinner was over and everyone began attempting to exit the marquee with more elements of it collapsing all the time.

Outside some enterprising wags had made an early exit. Making the most productive use of their time, they had found a fire hose, looped it through as many coaches as possible and waited in ambush. As people began streaming out of the collapsing marquee, the fire hose was turned on and aimed in their general direction. However, powerful fire hoses develop a mind of their own and as their prank had had the desired initial effect, the wags decided it was best to leg it. Free of any restraint whatsoever, the abandoned fire hose then proceeded to lash around in every direction, despite the best efforts of one or two game career officers who made valiant, but ultimately self-

defeating, efforts to bring it under control. Little did they know that the resourceful and intelligent wags had also gone to the trouble of sabotaging the water control after they had turned the hose on. Eventually, after all sorts of mayhem, everyone dispersed back onto the coaches and disappeared off into the night, including a large group of wet and very p***ed off VIPs.

Retribution was required and heads must roll following such a fiasco. But the sheer scale of events, the numbers involved and the difficulty of identifying individual culprits, created unique difficulties. Finally, it was decided that all those that attended would have a hat on, stand-up bollocking from their Station Commander, regardless of their involvement in certain activities or otherwise. The bollockings were duly administered and recorded in their next F1369.

I can vouch for the veracity of the above which of course covers only part of the mayhem.

CHAPTER 12 - To the North Pole and More

Dick, my new co-pilot, was one of the keenest individuals I've ever flown with. He was inquisitive of the aircraft's performance and its systems as well as its handling. Often, he had his nose in the Operating Data Manual (ODM) which contained enough graphs and tables to make a person dizzy. There were take-off and landing graphs, each with line after line covering every eventuality: wind; weight; temperature; airfield elevation; runway slope; normal or emergency braking, the point at which the brakes were likely to catch fire. There were graphs and tables for landing at normal weights, above normal weights, with the usual parameters of wind, temperature, etc. There were graphs about fuel consumption, range, endurance, cruise climbing etc. Dick would get his nose stuck in the ODM as thought it was a James Bond novel.

I had had an idea for some time which would make use of Dick's interest in the ODM. I thought it might be possible for a Vulcan to fly from a base in northern Norway, once around the north pole then back to the UK. Flight distance is about 4,200 miles which I thought possible carrying additional fuel in the bomb bay tank. Dick did a howgozit graph which showed, in no wind conditions, that it was indeed possible, landing back at Scampton well over the minimum landing fuel of 8,000 pounds. The most economical technique was cruise climbing, which

---

[12] Air Traffic Control is not keen on cruise climbing for safety reasons, as it is difficult to ensure vertical separation is maintained (unless you are Concorde starting the climb well above 50,000 feet where no one else flies).

entailed slowly increasing altitude as fuel is used and weight is reduced. [12]

We had to prove the accuracy of the Dick's work by preparing a very long Astro navigated trip over the Atlantic flying a large square box, gaining 1,000 feet at each corner to simulate cruise climbing. The graph was spot on (a reflection on the boffins at AVRO who produced the graphs). We flew for some 6 hours 55 minutes, which was a record[13] That 6:55 hours left us with sufficient fuel for nearly 45 minutes of flight and still land with the minimum. So, at an average speed of 600 mph we could easily make the trip. The other advantage, for safety's sake, as we flew back to Scampton we travelled down the east coast of the UK, where a plethora of airfields could be used as bolt holes.

This done, I prepared a report for approval by Number 1 Group staff. The report had the support of my squadron commander, but the response was: No! It would have been interesting for the navigation team particularly, because in the polar regions, magnetic compasses are unusable. The new ground position indicator which came with Blue Steel, had a facility just for that purpose. Vulcans, as it turned out, never did circumnavigate the North Pole.

****

---

[13] This record time was soon beaten by an 83 Squadron Flight Commander who did 7:05. On a different sortie he managed to climb the Vulcan well above 60,000 feet in spite of the 56,000 feet restriction.

I suppose I was lucky to have so few emergencies when I flew the Vulcan on 83 and 617 Squadrons. Other than one engine blowing up during a flying test when I was a co-pilot, my log book shows no major, and few minor failures right to the end of my tour as a captain. There was the odd single power flying control failure, an alternator or perhaps one of the artificial feel units packing up. These were minor problems and easy to handle. Contrast my luck with that of Bill T.'s, a squadron colleague on 617. It seemed that every time Bill got airborne, he would come back with a major failure or a number of minor ones: engines failed; multiple alternators failure; hydraulic pressure at zero necessitating the use of the emergency undercarriage lowering system (successful); and finally blowing up and burning a whole Vulcan on the threshold of runway 05 at Scampton. In a sense he was lucky in that no one in his crew nor any of his passengers ever got hurt. I suggested to my squadron commander that the RAF should give Bill £50,000 and ask him to leave the service. Although that attracted some laughs, it would have saved a deal of money as Bill's subsequent postings on Hunters and VC10s proved. But there again, nobody hurt.

****

Although we performed all types of attacks both with a ballistic bomb and Blue Steel, I can hardly remember what they consisted of except for the 2A attack mentioned above (the weave on the attack run) and the 2H pop-up manoeuvre, or maybe it was the 2F. The 2H, or 2F, attack was interesting and demanding. I experimented with the auto-throttles system to assist in carrying out this attack which, as it turned out, became altogether easier. Let me explain:

The auto-throttles maintained the speed at which it was engaged. It was possible to increase or decrease the speed by rotating a button on the auto-throttle control unit and indicator. (A large dial mounted on the left of the first pilot's main instrument panel). The system was engaged using a button just to the left of the throttle quadrant. It could maintain speed better than handling the throttles manually. Disengagement was by squeezing a small trigger mounted at the top of numbers one and four throttles. That was quite instinctive. However, the system was limited to a maximum of 180 knots. Above that speed, a bar dropped across the speed indicator dial partially obscuring the numbers, although they still remained readable and continue to show aircraft speed.

The pop-up attack was used as a means of delivering a weapon. It was particularly sensitive on speed accuracy. The attack consisted of approaching the target at low level at 350 knots. At a certain distance from the target, the nose was raised to a specific angle of climb (about +10 degrees) with a view to level off at 11,000 feet. (This was the manoeuvre used for bombing the Stanley runway during the Falklands dispute). As the manoeuvre started, all throttles were set to full power. Speed started decreasing but generally settled at about 320 knots. At the pushover, which started at about 10,500 feet to level at 11,000 feet, it was difficult to keep the speed steady, that is no acceleration nor deceleration. This was the co-pilot's job (the other pilot was busy keeping the wings absolutely level and maintaining an accurate altitude). It was rare to keep the speed steady as the push over took place. Even an experienced pilot found it very difficult to do. This could result in inaccurate bombing.

So, in spite of the 180 knots limitation, I decided to try to use the auto-throttles for a 2H attack. I had tested that it worked well above 180 knots, in fact all the way to 350 knots. Although this was some way outside the limit, the system operated very smoothly. For a 2H, or 2F, attack the system was engaged as we ran in at low level at 350kts. As we started the manoeuvre, automatically all throttles opened to full power. After a short while the speed settled around 320 knots and I disengaged the system. The auto-throttles speed indicator dropped to the speed we were climbing at. At that point I re-engaged the auto-throttles and as I started the push over, the system moved the throttles back and kept the speed within one knot. This was most impressive. We proved that it worked, improving our accuracy and making life much easier for the co-pilot and less worrying for the captain and the bomb aimer.

Having established the viability of the method, I submitted a paper to Number 1 Group via the squadron commander. I was lightly reprimanded by the boss saying that I used the system well outside its permitted parameter. Nevertheless, he approved my report and sent the paper off. I got quite a rocket from 1 Group. Rather than investigate the method's feasibility by further testing and trial flights at Boscombe Down, the whole idea was scotched. Indeed, the system was isolated and made unusable. I'm afraid this is the sort of reaction which I got time and time again from the authorities, for viable suggestions some easy to implement. Even those I made as an examiner. The answer always seemed to be NO!

CHAPTER 13 – Tour End and Central Flying School

I was coming to the end of my tour. As usual as tour end approaches, I was asked what I would like do next. I wanted to become a Vulcan flying instructor on 230 OCU. My boss Bob Allen strongly supported my suggestion and so did Number 1 Group. I was delighted. What came next was a bit of a shock though.

The RAF would not accept my RCAF instructor's qualifications although the standards and course contents were exactly the same as the RAF's, and I still had the documentation. (The RCAF system was standardised and checked by the RAF Central Flying School). There was no choice however, I had to do a refresher course on Jet Provost (JP) at RAF Manby near Louth in Lincolnshire from the end of January 1968 to the beginning of March. Our daughter Michelle was born on 28 February. I commuted every day and took a few days leave when Michelle was born. My colleagues on the course sent Carole congratulatory flowers which were deeply appreciated.

As soon as I finished the JP course, I was posted to Little Rissington in Gloucestershire, some 125 miles from home. This was a very fraught period for us. I had to live in the mess during the week and travel home only at weekends. Allowances in those days were poor. Living in the mess meant I had to pay a mess bill every month which was a considerable amount. Travel allowances were paid at a measly rate for just one return trip home a month. Salaries were not generous and Carole had to stop working towards the end of her pregnancy. There was no maternity leave, paid or otherwise.

In addition, I did not like the JP (I'm not sure it liked me) chiefly because of the layout of the cockpit. In the training aircraft I was used to and liked, tandem seating was the arrangements I much preferred, like the Chipmunk, the Harvard and the T33. In the JP it was a side-by-side seating layout. The student pilot felt he was being spied on (which he was) by the instructor sitting beside him. Nevertheless, I went on with all the required exercises in the course. They were much the same as the Harvard course I had experienced and taught in the RCAF in the Harvard. The JP was good in aerobatics. Some manoeuvres I found difficult such as stall turns, and the point rolls where the nose stayed pointing at the horizon.[14] I also quite liked zero-g pushovers when I tried to keep my glove floating in the cockpit as stationary and for as long as possible. Some people experienced zero-g for very much longer in a converted Airbus aircraft nicknamed the Vomit Comet.

Towards the end of the course I was asked, like all my course mates, which Flying Training School I would like to go to. "I'm going back to 230 OCU on Vulcans", I replied. "No! All graduates from the QFI training course are posted to an FTS". I was deeply concerned. Having already flown over 1,500 instructional hours under my belt, albeit on Harvards, I was

---

[14] I was used to aileron rolls where only ailerons were used resulting in the nose dropping throughout the manoeuvre. I was shown an RAF-type roll when I was instructing in the RCAF. In this manoeuvre, the rudder is used to keep the nose from dropping below the horizon, or whichever point is chosen. I did not like being cross-controlled at all.

determined not to go back to training pilots from scratch. I phoned the OC 617 squadron, Bob Allen, to ask for his support. I told him that I was willing to resign my commission if I was posted to an FTS. Bob took it up with Number 1 Group. An administrative battle between 1 Group - supported by Bomber Command - with Training Command ensued. The upshot would be that if I did not get back to 230 OCU, I would be withdrawn from the course and return to 617 Squadron. Number 1 Group won. I ended up at RAF Finningley as a Vulcan QFI. My end of course assessment was that I was proficient. A remark was added by the flight commander who had been posted to Vulcans. He would see how good an instructor I was on Vulcans as he expected to be my first student. As it turned out he went to fly Victors.

CHAPTER 14 - 230 Operational Conversion Unit - Qualified Flying Instructor

I arrived on the OCU on the 29th June 1968 with a big smile on my face. Once all the administrations tasks were complete, I set out to learn the syllabus used to teach students to fly the Vulcan. There were a couple of exceptional instructors on the OCU at the time, one of whom I've already mentioned, John Stannard. I started the conversion course to obtain my qualification as QFI on Vulcans. The first sortie was just to get my hand back in. There was no problem there. Flying the Vulcan was so ingrained in me that it was the equivalent of having learned to ride a bike. This was a very quiet period on the OCU. Few crews needed training so it gave me the opportunity to fly ordinary training sorties and ease the pressure on getting my qualifications as Vulcan QFI. I had lots of practice and much fun flying with rear crews who were all ground school and flying navigation/bombing, and electronics instructors. After quite some time, my final handling took place with the Chief Instructor in two separate sorties as there was insufficient fuel to cover all that he required in one trip. The second sortie was quite short at just under 1:30 hour doing circuits and roller landing on the 6,000 runway at RAF Lindholme just north of Finningley.

****

Like all new instructors I started my Vulcan instructional career with a B2 category. And it was as such that I got my first student. He was a co-pilot on an Intermediate Co-pilot's Course

(ICC) which was really both a checkout in the left-hand seat, and an assessment of captaincy potential. Most of these trips were quite short, carrying just one navigator and an AEO, as all the work concentrated on the student. I enjoyed cutting my Vulcan QFI teeth with this student. He passed and eventually got a captaincy.

My first student full crew was in February 1969. I took a young Chris Lumb through the course successfully. (He went on to command 101 squadron at Waddington a few years later. Then as a Station Commander at Brize Norton). For a Vulcan QFI, teaching a crew completely new to the aircraft was demanding. In spite of the experience the crew had gained from the various flight, navigation and electronics simulators, we gave extensive pre-flight ground briefings, usually the day before, taking up to 90 minutes and going into great details of the forthcoming sortie.

On the day the flight took place, the crew and the instructor came in some three hours before take-off for pre-flight planning and briefing. For the first two exercises, the QFI started talking nearly on arrival, and to be truthful, talked for most of the time for the next 7 hours. For a new crew on the Vulcan, there was a lot to explain and to demonstrate. The pilots started at the met office for a weather briefing. Then the state of the aircraft was checked followed by reading the appropriate NOTAMS (Notice to Airmen) which indicated the state of the airfield, the airspace we were planning to use and, particularly, restrictions which may affect the sortie; ensure the flight was correctly authorised (all QFIs on the OCU authorised their own flights. Most crews on a squadron were authorised by a flight commander or the boss). The navigators, together with their instructors, would be drawing lines of a chart, look at the likely radar images of the target and so on. The AEO would write up his communications plan, and at the end of all this planning and checking, the captain was expected to give a briefing. The instructors then added specific information dealing with their intentions. Then off we went for a pre-flight meal.

Once we were told our aircraft was ready, we'd change into our flying clothing which took some 15 minutes, making sure all the equipment we carried; oxygen mask, connectors; bone dome (helmet); immersion suit were checked and serviceable. Then off in a crew coach to the dispersal where the aircraft log was checked and signed. From that point, I was responsible for the aircraft and what happened to it. Vulcan external visual checks were few but it was good to walk around the aircraft and ensure that all ground equipment was correctly positioned. Normally the captain was the last to climb aboard, by which time, the rear crew were installed in their seats, and the co-pilot in his, although not strapped in. As QFI with a trainee captain I sat in the right-hand seat and carried out co-pilot duties. The first pilot was at least familiar with strapping in from practices in the flight simulator. Both pilots were helped by the aircraft servicing chief (crew chief) who would also make the ejection seats and the canopy live. When ready the first pilot called for the checklist. The AEO read each challenge and ensured a correct response. The checklist was extensive and took at least half an hour to get through to engine start. With the engines running, a few more checks were carried out before closing the entrance door and obtaining taxy clearance.

When the first pilot had no experience of taxying, I demonstrated the use of brakes and nose wheel steering on the way to the runway. Steering the Vulcan on the ground could be interesting chiefly because there were a number of ways to steer it, one easy and all the rest awkward. The nosewheel steering button at the bottom of the control column was used in conjunction with rudder pedal deflection. Turning circles were good and could be helped with a dab of brakes. The aircraft could easily turn around in a 200-foot-wide runway. It was possible, with care, to do a 180 degree turn on a 150-foot-wide runway. The taxiways were 35 feet wide and at night, the centre line was lit with green lights set in the surface. Normally we taxied at a fast-walking pace. In both Finningley and later in Scampton, there could be well over one mile of taxying to reach the runway. This was a good opportunity to demonstrate and practice taxying.

Once at the holding point just short of the runway, the last of the pre-take-off checks were done which included a crew pre-take-off briefing. The briefing covered actions to take in case of emergencies. After which the crew checked in confirming their understanding of the brief and that they were ready for take-off. The aircraft was then lined up on the runway. For newcomers the take-off was quite an experience. Because OCU sorties were relatively short – there is only so much a student crew can absorb – we carried only 80% of the full fuel load, making the aircraft considerably lighter.

So off we go. Initially, the throttles, under the control of the pilot carrying out the take-off are open to 80% engine RPM, at which point temperatures and pressures are checked. The brakes are released and full power applied. Because the nose wheel steering button is at the bottom of the control column, and at the same time the control column must be pushed a few inches forward to stop the nose rising too early (this action required two hands), control of the throttles was given to the other pilot. Speeds were called by the navigator plotter every 10 knots, calling "rotate" at the appropriate speed. The pilot raised the nose to a pre-set position on the artificial horizon.

Once airborne, the brakes were applied for four seconds to stop the wheels rotating before bringing the undercarriage up.[15] As long as the undercarriage was fully up by 200 knots, all was fine. The speed quickly built up to 250 knots, the normal climbing speed. Operational climb speed was 300 knots and although it got the aircraft to altitude more quickly more fuel was used. Passing 20,000 feet, the nose was lowered gently a few degrees to let the speed increase to 300 knots which was maintained until an indicated Mach number (IMN) of 0.86 was reached at about 33,000 feet. From that altitude up, cruise speed was 0.86 IMN, an actual Mach 0.84.

Some 10 minutes after take-off, our cruising altitude was reached which was usually between 41,000 and 45,000 feet.[16]

---

[15] This was due to the Dunlop Maxaret anti-skid system, which was a mechanical arrangement and very effective, but the wheels kept rotating even when the brakes were applied because there was no deceleration felt by the system. After about 4 seconds, the wheels stopped.

[16] In aviation parlance, above a certain height, altitudes are called Flight Levels. So,

The top of the climb checks were done and I, as co-pilot, did a full fuel check at the same time as supervising how my student sitting next to me did. For some students, this was a first time. The Vulcan handling at all levels was a joy. It was pleasant and rewarding to see a student enjoy himself. For a new rear crew, using the equipment for real was interesting and demanding.

We usually set off at high level on a heading of about 340 degrees under RAF radar control until the late 1960s when the UK air traffic system started to take over most of the UK airspace. RAF radar units were then kept busy otherwise. There were a number of demonstrations at high level which included steep turns (quite demanding but rewarding if, after turning through 360 degrees, there was a slight bump as we flew through our own slipstream). We also flew with some of the many stabilisation aids turned off, as well as with one of the powered flying controls inoperative. One of the manoeuvres was a Dutch Roll which most pilots had heard or read about but never experienced. To provoke a Dutch Roll, the yaw damper (a very effective stability aid) was turned off and much rudder was applied keeping the wings level. Normally when the rudder is released, the aircraft return to straight flight, as it does so it banks in the same direction as the yaw: that is yaw left, bank left. The exact opposite occurs in the Vulcan, yaw left, bank right. Because the Yaw Damper is off, the yawing continues back and forth for some time. During the manoeuvre, the Yaw Damper is turned back on, and nearly instantly, the aircraft settles in straight flight. It was always good fun to demonstrate

---

43,000 feet was FL430.

this. The rear crew was warned to ensure that articles such as pencils and pens did not become loose articles in the cabin as substantial side forces were applied with the rudder.

By the time that last demonstration was complete, we had reached Wick in the north of Scotland and time to turn round and head back south. We would then carry out high speed runs to 0.93 IMN. The Vulcan became unstable approaching the speed of sound. Above about 0.88 IMN, the nose tended to tuck under. If the speed was increased further, the nose tucked under increasingly. Although this tuck-under could be controlled by the elevators, at about 0.96 IMN the elevators were fully up and control would be lost. This was a dangerous situation which was dealt with by a system called Automatic Mach Trimmers. These would feed an excess of up elevator as the speed increased above 0.88 IMN forcing the pilot to push on the control column to maintain level flight. The push got stronger as the speed increased. This of course is exactly what a pilot expects of an aircraft as the speed increases. We were limited to 0.93 IMN so that we never approached dangerous, instability, speeds. This demonstration included high speed runs without the Mach trimmers. This gave valuable experience of the danger of excessive speed as the pull to maintain control in level flight was considerable.

The rest of the leg southward was to prepare for the crew's first simulated bomb run under the control of the navigators, mainly the navigator radar. It was not a difficult exercise for the pilots as it was nearly all straight and level flight.

Rather than return to base, we would go into our allocated area to demonstrate low speed handling. This consisted of handling the aircraft at circuits speeds, and indeed flying a few imaginary circuits with a runway at 2000 feet above the surface. The need for rudder input became quite obvious when selecting large amounts of aileron to initiate turns. The induced yaw was more than just considerable, hence the reason for a boot full of rudder just ahead of feeding in the ailerons. Once all this was over, including reducing speed to the minimum of 115 (could be higher depending on the weight), we returned to the circuit where real work, both of the instructor and the student pilot started. It was fun to observe after the demonstration by the instructor, how the first circuit by the student was well flown frequently ending up in a good landing. But the second circuit often resulted in the sort of landing felt by everyone on board. I think that first circuit was better than the subsequent one because pilots tended to let their instinct fly the circuit and landing. But the second time, they've had time to analyse what they did and tried to override instincts. A series of instrument and visual approaches were carried out terminating by a landing using the tail brake parachute. There was a definite technique to use here because if the parachute was deployed when the nose wheel was still off the ground, it would smash it down most firmly. Although with practice it was possible to stop that happening, it was a method never taught.

So, home to dispersal, tell the technicians the faults which emerged during the flight, sign the book and get back to operations for a shower and a crew debrief which normally was short. Each instructor would then sit with his student and talk the trip through. For the pilots, this could take a good 30 or 40 minutes. That was the point when I just about stopped talking. I had been doing so, on and off (on mainly), for the last 8 hours and it was time to go home. A student pilot new to the aircraft, was pretty exhausted by then, and nearly always exhilarated. That is the sort of aircraft the Vulcan was.

If the weather was suitable the following day, we did a repeat flight, exercise 2, this time with the co-pilot and the other navigator. The AEO was still supervised with additional duties for him to carry out. But the general profile of the flight was much the same with the exception that the co-pilot only did one or two circuits. These periods in the circuit were much more enjoyable for the QFI and sometimes I did a few more circuits just for the pleasure of it.

Another half day's briefing followed in preparation for exercises 3 and 4, which dealt primarily with asymmetric flight and descending the aircraft rapidly simulating a sudden cabin depressurisation. At the same time. it was a good opportunity to review the two previous flights.

The sortie following the ground briefing was chiefly to get practice for the captain and for me, a demonstration of asymmetric flight starting at about 2000 ft. At high level it was the usual handling of steep turns, high speed runs and of course some simulated bomb runs. The asymmetric demo took place initially over the Humber (I saw the Humber bridge being built over the years) and included using full power on two engines on one side to show the minimum speed at which the Vulcan could be controlled when asymmetric. We returned to the circuit to demonstrate a simulated asymmetric circuit and overshoot. It was important to decide whether to land or go-round at or over 200 feet above ground. Any lower was dangerous as there may be insufficient altitude to carry out the manoeuvre. Once committed however, full airbrakes were selected and the speed allowed to bleed slowly back by 10 knots as we crossed the threshold of the runway. Rollers from simulated asymmetric approaches were only permitted by a QFI as there had been a few accidents and not a few incidents when squadron captains attempted to roll from an asymmetric approach.

The next exercise was conversion to night flying in the Vulcan for both pilots. The sorties were quite straight forward and generally good value. After one more crew solo the Final Handling test took place normally with the Chief Flying Instructor or the Chief Instructor. I don't remember if a crew ever failed. Perhaps flying the Vulcan was easy, after all.

CHAPTER 15 - Aircraft Modifications/Additions

Any new aircraft coming into service is bound to have a few defects. Also, the parameters of its use change. These changes generate modifications, some of which are entirely technical and aircrew may know nothing about them, which is perhaps just as well. There are some modifications which affect handling, use, and may improve the aircraft altogether. For example, the Vulcan was initially equipped with a facility to aid its take-off by using rockets installed under the back of the fuselage. RATOG or Rocket Assisted Take-off Gear. There was a large lever positioned on the instrument panel above the fuel console to activate the system. The rocket system was never fitted and the lever was removed. This created the ideal position for a navigation instrument called TACAN, or Tactical Air Navigation, which was extensively used for point-to-point navigation as well as being a crucial aid for arriving or departing many military and civilian airfields. Accurate interpretation of use of TACAN took some training.

Blue Steel was fitted to the Vulcan in the early 1960s. The fitting required major modifications to the aircraft bomb bay doors with additional equipment installed on the bomb bay walls. Although there were few additions or changes for the pilots, a much-improved navigation ground position indicator (GPI6) was added for the navigation team. However, Blue Steel also brought plenty of problems for technicians as well as aircrew.

In the early 1960s, the British government was interested in a development that a US company was working on: a medium range air-launched ballistic missile; Skybolt. Two would be carried under the Vulcan wings. The aircraft was modified during production to strengthen the wing attachment points as each missile would weigh about 10,000 lbs. Skybolt and some Blue steel modifications introduced more powerful engines, the 301 series with some 21,000 lbs of thrust. In addition, modifications were made allowing for a rapid engine start system, using compressed air. The compass and artificial horizon were modified to produce very quick gyro erection when using the engine rapid start. Rapid start also started the power flying controls, all the stabilisation aids and the artificial feel system. All this produced an aircraft which, when on alert, could be airborne in less than a minute after the scramble message. Not even fighter aircraft could beat that. Skybolt was cancelled but the modifications made the Vulcan stronger, allowing it to keep flying at low level without unduly using up fatigue life. Skybolt attachment points on each wing were used to carry anti-radar missiles and jamming pods during the Falklands dispute.

Vulcan carrying 2 Skybolt dummy missiles

From the middle to the end of the 1960s, Terrain Following Radar was introduced (TFR). The Vulcan was one of the first aircraft to use TFR and although we appreciated its great advantage, we were wary of its fragility and faults. This was all analogue electronics and at times, temperamental. When TFR was first fitted to an aircraft, a lengthy flight test was required to calibrate the angle of attack vanes (AoA) fitted on either side of the front fuselage. The information from the AoA was fed to radar output which came from a small radar unit on the nose of the aircraft. Pitch demands were shown on the artificial horizon (termed director horizon) which, if followed would fly the aircraft accurately following contours. It was fairly reliable but when it failed, it could direct the pilot to fly into the ground or water. Practicing flying with TRF needed good weather and a good lookout by the other pilot.

Before a route could be flown using TFR, a check on the hill contours was required (normally carried out by senior, experienced staff) to ensure that the pilots were aware of a situation where a hill of a little lower elevation was behind the hill being climbed. In that event if TFR demands were followed, the aircraft could fly dangerously closer to second hill top than the selected height (between 200 ft and 1000 ft). Eventually, a warning light was installed in front of the first pilot which, when it came on, indicated a failure (called the "I've become suicidal warning light"). Pilots then and ignored the demands and went back to visual flying.

Squadrons equipped with Blue Steel were glad to see the back of it in 1970, but the aircraft retained the navigation kit that had come with the missile. Nuclear weapons had shrunk a great deal during the life of the Vulcan. The bomb bay was enormous (the Victor bomb bay even bigger) to accommodate the British designed weapon, Yellow Sun, which at 21 feet long and 4 feet in diameter fitted snugly.

Yellow Sun

Eventually Yellow sun was replaced by a much smaller weapon, the W177 which looked like a large 1000 lbs iron bomb but it weighted about 2,000lbs.

WE177 nuclear weapon

The Vulcan could carry 21 thousand pounds bombs of the type used to attack the runway at Stanley during the Falklands dispute: The only time the Vulcan was used in anger.

20 thousand-pound bombs (plus 1 below the frame)

CHAPTER 16 – Stories

In the mid-60s a series of amusing flight safety posters were published. Some were for aircrew some for technical staff. In that series Fred was the star. Fred was a British Rail wheel tapper. With his special hammer, he tapped every train wheel that came into the station. British Rail changed 776 wheels before they found out Fred's hammer was cracked. The lesson was "Ensure your instruments are calibrated". In another poster, Fred had an apprentice. He instructed him "When I nod me 'ead, 'it it". When Fred nodded his apprentice knocked him unconscious. The lesson, was to ensure instructions are clear and unambiguous. Which brings me to my story:

I was instructing a co-pilot who was doing the Intermediate Co-pilot Course. We were flying at high level at the start of a simulated bomb run, some 60 miles from the target. In the Vulcan, whenever the CofG indicator button was pressed, all fuel gauges needles dropped to zero. This also happened when, in an emergency, the electrical non-essential loads were shed. The student in the left-hand seat saw the gauges drop to zero and asked the AEO is he had shed the non-essential loads. All the AEO heard, was "Shed the non-essential loads", which he promptly did. When these loads are shed, all the navigation gear stops which did not please the navigation team at the start of their bombing run. To reset the loads, a series of check had to be carried out. These were done in double-quick time, the loads were reset and the navigation gear restarted. Of all the luck, we had a direct hit on the target. Still, it certainly was a lesson for the student to be clear and appropriate in his instructions.

Another poster appeared with, this time, a rather funny looking creature which the poster called "A Flat-Billed, Multi-Fingered Switch Flicker (FMSF). The sort of individual who says, "I wonder that this is for?" as he presses the button, or flicks the switch. I must say that perhaps the label fits me a little. I was always very inquisitive and keen to take things apart and mostly put them back together, at times not always successfully. One could not be an FMSF in a Vulcan. But some aspects were worth exploring. I told the story previously of my unusual out-of-the-limits use of the auto-throttles.

This time it has to do with the automatic Mach-trimmers. I've explained before why Mach-trimmers were required in the Vulcan. Each auto-mach trimmers was controlled by a simple button; pulled for on and push for off. A blue light came on in the button when the trimmers were feeding up elevators. If the light was on and the button was pushed feeding more up elevator would stop but the controls remained in the relative position they had moved to. When we did high-speed runs, we did not trim the elevators but simply pushed the stick to maintain height. I decided to play around with the AMTs to see if I could get the aircraft to fly at say, 0.90M, in trim, but without using the trimming system (the multi-direction button on top of the stick). I accelerated to 0.90M having switched off one Mach trimmer. The forces on the stick were negligible. So that seemed to work. I went a bit faster and as the aircraft accelerated, I switched on the other the trimmer for just a second, then off again. That removed any out-of-trim force. So, I found out the way to fly at high speed without effort and the other advantage is that as I engaged the autopilot, the system behaved perfectly well. There was nothing dangerous in what I did. I liked experimenting and exploring. I kept that information to myself. I just told the crew we were doing a high-speed run. The co-pilot was also a QFI and knew what I was doing, but kept it to himself too.

****

It was a night instructional sortie for the trainee captain in the left-hand seat. The trip had gone well and the Vulcan was back in the circuit. After a few instrument circuits, a number of visual circuits were carried out. Soon after rolling (touch and go) on the last visual circuits, the QFI throttled back a pair of engines to simulate a double engine failure on one side. The first action in these circumstances is reduce drag. The undercarriage was raised and the visual circuit continued. (During normal circuit work in the Vulcan, the undercarriage is left down to save wear and tear.)

The undercarriage indicator brightness (green, red) can be dimmed at night. The downwind checks were carried out as normal, the first one being "Undercarriage?" to which the response is "Down with three greens". That was the response the QFI gave, believed by the first pilot in the left -hand seat busy controlling the aircraft. The response was entirely instinctive but wrong because the wheels were still up. In spite of the usual call by the pilot to the tower just to obtain landing permission: "Finals, three greens", the wheels remained up. At night the air traffic controller could not see the state of the aircraft and gave landing clearance.   A wheels-up landing followed.

I don't know what happened to the QFI, but the aircraft was not badly damaged (airbrakes and the metal posts on which they stood were worn out, as well as quite a few scratches under the fuselage!).[17]

****

When Neil McDougall did his last air-to-air refuelling on his way back from a Falklands Dispute Black Buck mission, the refuelling probe broke. He was left with enough fuel to either ditch in the Atlantic or try to get to Rio, in Brazil. To Rio it was. Except that the Brazilian would not allow his aircraft to enter Brazilian airspace in spite of repeating his mayday calls saying this was a 4-jet aircraft short of fuel, in emergency, requesting to land in Rio. Eventually the controller asked for the Vulcan's departure airfield. Much thought was given to this question. It was not a good idea to say Ascension Island. One of the navigators suggested "Tell them we're from Huddersfield". This information was duly transmitted to the Brazilian controller who, I imagine, opened his book of airfields searching for Huddersfield. By the time he closed his book, the aircraft had landed. It was tucked away in a corner of the airfield. Brazil was too busy getting ready for a Papal visit.

---

[17] In similar circumstances I too gave the response "Down with three greens" going downwind when the wheels were up. For just an instant, I saw three green lights. But the lesson above had had an effect because I always double checked the state of the undercarriage. "No! They're up" I nearly yelled, and lowered the wheels. We landed normally. Phew!

Early in the Vulcan's life, the powers that be thought that a navigator or an AEO could be captain rather than a pilot. So, it was tried. Experimentally, of course. A navigator plotter of Squadron Leader rank was designated as captain. After all, in other Commands, aircraft captains were not necessarily pilots. But in the V-Force, the navigator plotter was perhaps the busiest man in the crew. If in addition he had captaincy responsivities...

The first pilot was resentful of this arrangement and worked out a ploy to prove that in a V-Bomber at least, only a pilot could be captain. Incidentally, when crew positions were called, they were First Pilot, Co-Pilot, Radar, Plotter and AE. If and when the term Captain was used as identification, it was likely to be the result of a serious decision, possibly during an emergency. For example, "Captain to crew, prepare for ditching!"

In the experimental try-out, on the crew's first solo, the first pilot held his counsel until recovery to the airfield began when he announced "First-pilot to captain, I'd like to stream the tail braking chute on landing". "Very well", replied the captain, "stream the 'chute". Half way through the descent from some 40,000 feet, the first pilot said he had changed his mind and did not want to stream the 'chute, a decision with which the captain agreed. Going downwind in the circuit, the first-pilot said that he would like to stream the chute after all. This was agreed once more, until on final approach the fist-pilot changed his mind yet again, not to stream the 'chute. The captain, I expect, bored by all this indecision agreed. As the aircraft touched down the first-pilot announced "Pilot's decision, I'm streaming the 'chute". The experiment failed.

CHAPTER 17 – Various

When the OCU moved from RAF Finningley to RAF Scampton, QFIs started to use the area along the river Trent for asymmetric demonstrations. It was useful as there are three very large power stations along the river which made it more difficult for the pilots to get lost! A Vulcan at full power at 2000 feet above ground (even when using only two engines) was very noisy. It was not long before residents of villages along the river started to complain. We had to move again. We could no longer use the Humber as the Bridge was near completion, so we were shifted to a few miles off Flamborough Head over the North Sea. This was quite some distance from Scampton so we had to think of something useful that would keep the crew busy for the recovery back to base. Together with another QFI, we designed an instrument arrival procedure using the TACAN, which eventually was adopted officially by the UK Air Traffic System.

* * * * * * * * * *

This was my first tour as a QFI on the OCU. Like every officer I was given a secondary duty: assistant to the Public Relations Officer. An easy and at times pleasant small job. Every year in September the station, like many RAF stations, put on an air display to commemorate the Battle of Britain. In 1969 RAF Finningley hosted the French aerobatic team, La Patrouille de France. La Patrouille arrived on Thursday before the air display. It consisted of 7 Fougat Magister trainers (tandem seating of course) and a Nord Atlas, an elderly twin-engine transport. Being a French speaker, indeed an official British Civil Service

Interpreter (for which I was awarded £100 when I took the examination), I was detailed to look after the whole lot of French Air Force, pilots, engineers, technicians and hangers on. It was not a difficult job. In fact, rather enjoyable. As they arrived, they taxied into one of the dispersals, the formation leader in the first aircraft. As he went by with his oxygen mask off his face, I saw what I can only describe as a unique nose, one I had not seen since my pilot training in Canada in 1955. Could it possibly be Hector Pissochet? The nose did not disappoint me. It was indeed Hector, leading La Patrouille, like me still just a Captain and as loud as ever with his amazing bass voice. It was a most pleasant coincidence. In 1955, he and 9 other French Air Force student pilots had been on my course, number 5508 in Alberta and Manitoba. We talked about the others. He'd lost track of most who had probably left the Air Force (National Service was in force in France) but two individuals we remembered, Geoffroy and Chapel. Geoffroy was in jail, which did not surprise me, but Chapel, who had been a 2nd Lieutenant (the others were all sergeants) was, after just 14 years, a general!

The following day, Friday, the team did a rehearsal which nearly resulted in a major accident. As one aircraft formatted inverted above another Fougat, the upper aircraft canopy flew off, just missing the other. Another display practice took place later in the day using the spare Fougat. I lunched with the team on the actual air display day. I was surprised that they all had a glass of wine with their lunch which was just a couple of hours before they were due to fly. This was very much against RAF rules. The FAF obviously operated differently. The team left after the formal display finished, returning to their base in the Champagne region but leaving behind a couple of cases of fine Champagne.

****

As Assistant PR Officer, I was once tasked to host a BBC TV production team making a series, one episode of which required a Vulcan taxying and taking off. The taxying bit was easy as OCU aircraft were frequently coming in and out of dispersal. However, the take-off sequence was more awkward as the cameraman had to be quite close to the runway at the 'rotate' point.

I arranged with air traffic to position the cameraman at about 2,500 feet from the beginning of the runway opposite the area where most Vulcans got airborne and about 20 feet from the runway edge. I warned the director that the noise would be very, very loud that close to the four jet pipes. I was assured that the cameraman would be wearing the equivalent of ear defenders (they were just earphones plugged into the camera). The Vulcan started its take-off run and the camera followed the aircraft faithfully all the way into its climb. There was no further movement from the cameraman. We approached him and as we did so, he took off his earphones and said, "I've never been so bl**dy frightened in my life by a noise like that." Well, they were warned

****

There were nine Vulcan Mk2 squadrons, 7 in the UK and 2 in Cyprus. This made a total of nearly 500 aircrew plus of course all those who needed familiarity with the aircraft such as Station Commanders, Officers Commanding Flying (in charge of Operations and the day-to-day management of flying services), Senior Air Staff Officers, Number 1 Group (usually an Air Commodore) and of course the Air Officer Commanding Number 1 Group, an Air Vice- Marshal. The number of OCU staff was considerable to cover aircraft and equipment conversion which was the sole purpose of the unit. Final role conversion, ballistic bombs, Blue Steel and eventually maritime reconnaissance, was done at squadron level. During my first tour as a QFI on 230, the majority of Captains had Vulcan experience. Most of the instruction was for the benefit of the co-pilot, and any rear crew member new to the aircraft. Often short courses were organised for partially experienced crew. Occasionally, brand new crews needed training which made a QFI's life much more interesting if somewhat tiring. There were very senior people to train too. They came often with little or no experience on large aircraft, let alone something like the Vulcan. OCU QFIs did not volunteer to teach VIPs. I must have been the last of a line of some 7 or 8 QFIs to be asked to instruct VIPs. The others having said "No, thank you", so I was volunteered! This turned out to be quite a good thing.

****

I instructed some superb, instinctive pilots. One in particularly comes to mind, Harry Nelson, who was completely new to the aircraft, still a Flying Officer having completed a tour

110

as a QFI on Jet Provost. It is difficult to describe the native ability, leadership and skill of Harry. If I demonstrated a manoeuvre such as, for example, a steep turn, he would do his better than I did. When we covered asymmetric flying, with which he was not very familiar, he understood the control problems and flew the Vulcan like an old hand. I believe Harry did not stay long on a squadron. He completed the course at the Empire Test Pilot School and eventually worked for Avro involved in the Vulcan tanker modification.

Another fine pilot was Air Commodore David Craig (who went on to be Commander-in-Chief Strike Command, Chief of the Air Staff, Chief of the Defence Staff, then Lord Craig). His flying was always immaculate and precise. One day I had briefed him on flying the asymmetric circuit. The morning we flew, he said he wanted to revise the briefing I had given him. He drew the diagram with one small error which I pointed out. "But that is the way you drew it yesterday". I had to admit to my mistake and asked if by any chance he had a photographic memory. He has. I was subsequently very careful what I drew and said.

Between instructing full courses, I was given a few interesting VIPs to teach, among who were the station commanders at Waddington and at Akrotiri, and the new AOC, Number 1 Group, AVM Peter Horsley. AVM Horsley flew mainly fighter aircraft. During the war he flew Mosquitoes in the ground attack role. He had limited experience of large aircraft, let alone the Vulcan. We started the conversion together in the simulator to familiarise him with the Vulcan cockpit. We did our first flight on the 30th December 1970. He was to be in post by mid-January giving him just over two weeks to complete the course. The long-term weather forecast was poor so I suggested we finish the course in Cyprus (he had been station commander there a few years earlier). This was instantly agreed with and organised. We departed on the 2nd January 1971 as a combination transit flight and the second exercise. We did the rest of the required exercises returning to the UK on the 9th January (for that last trip, I strongly suggested that he act as the aircraft captain, to which he agreed), leaving him plenty of time before taking over Number 1 Group. He was a good student and a capable pilot. We got along very well. He filled our evenings eating in his favourite restaurants in Limassol, with hilarious stories of the period he was equerry to Princess Elizabeth then to the Queen. He also told us of his being shot down in a Mosquito during the war. He drifted in his dinghy in the English Channel for three days in fog and then through a storm before being picked up by an RAF rescue launch. How lucky! I think he believed in ghosts (In fact, he writes as though convinced of the paranormal in his book *Sounds From Another Room)*.

CHAPTER 18 - A Failure and a Fly Past

The Chief Instructor, our boss, Wg Cdr Frank McClory[18] thought I should try for an A1 QFI category. A1 instructors are a bit like gold dust in the RAF. They are held in very high esteem. I only knew one such, Reg W. The depth of his knowledge, his ability and skill were astounding. I thought that since I did not want promotion, an A1 QFI status would do. I started studying for the ground oral examination. I was lucky in that a rare A1 instructor offered some personal tuition in meteorology and in jet aircraft range and endurance. I spent two days with him accumulating much knowledge about both these subjects.

I had to prepare a ground lecture to give to the staff at Central Flying School at Little Rissington. I was given a choice of two subjects: asymmetric flying or the Vulcan fuel system. Like a complete fool I chose asymmetric flying when there was so much material about the Vulcan fuel system in ground school than I could have equipped myself with all the slides and samples I could possibly need. Not only that but I knew the fuel system like the back of my hand. I made a hash of the asymmetric presentation. This upset me and the rest of the test was not up to my standard, let alone what CFS expected. I regret that stupid decision to this day. And I also regret letting down the boss who had much faith in me.

---

[18] Frank McClory was once walking through the instructors' staff room where we had been discussing how we could show our students that an aircraft on asymmetric power does not fly straight but with a slight lateral motion. We had really been scratching our collective heads. The boss very simply showed us how this happens using a packet of cigarettes. I must admit I had never seen a more convincing and short demonstration before.

****

In May and June 1970, I was involved in the lead aircraft for the Queen's Birthday flypast. The formation of some 16 aircraft was somewhat unwieldy and bitty since the 8 Lightnings which formatted on two of the Vulcans were so limited in their fuel endurance that they could not join us until we were about to turn onto the final leg some distance to the east of our target, Buckingham Palace. The rest of us, 3 Vulcans, 4 Phantoms and a Nimrod had no such problem. They formed up just to the north of Scampton. Tracking and timing was crucial. Both navigators worked on the tracking with some occasional visual assistance from the flight deck. Timing was chiefly by using position lines from the many runways of disused airfields over East Anglia (these have chiefly disappeared now as agricultural land or housing estates). Rehearsals stopped at Fairlop some 10 miles away from our target. Even in good visibility it was nearly impossible to pick out the Mall or Buck House from that distance at 1000 feet above ground. On the day of the fly past, 13th June, the weather was fine and the visibility was very good. The navigator radar identified Buckingham Palace and gave us a heading to steer. Soon I picked up the Palace visually. We were heading straight for it, over Admiralty Arch, the Mall, the Victoria Monument and we were there. A few seconds late, but just after Big Ben had bonged 1 o'clock. We turned back home over Bentley Priory, Fighter Command Headquarters. (I don't think anyone was watching other than a photographer) The formation soon broke up and we all went back home. We returned to a congratulatory signal from C-in-C, Strike Command. It was a

114

nerve-wracking exercise, which, as it turned out, we were so good at, we were asked to do it again the following year, 1971, with much the same results. I was told, I don't know how true it is, that the following year, the formation overflew Piccadilly and Marble Arch. I can visualise the royals on the Buck House balcony looking left and leaning forward to see the formation.

Queen's Birthday Fly Past 1970

****

Scrutinising all those names in my logbook during my first tour as a QFI on 230 OCU, pilots, navigators and AEOs, but mainly pilots, I note that some of them have reached high and some very high office in the RAF hierarchy. The first that appears in my log book is Fg Off Chris Lumb (mentioned previously) on February 5th 1969 doing exercise 1 on a captain's course. He got up to Group Captain, commanding RAF Lyneham.

Then Gordon Rayfield in April '69, to Wing Commander. In October '70, Flt Lt Peter Harding who managed to get to the very top as Chief of the Air Staff. In November '70 with Fg Off Ian Valance on exercise 2 as a co-pilot. He achieved Air-Vice-Marshal. In my days as co-pilot another co-pilot on the same squadron, Mike Pilkington who ended up as C-in-C Training Command as Air Marshal Sir Michael. Another two co-pilots, Ian Junor to Group Captain and Keith Walters the same. Then me, thankfully remaining a Flight Lieutenant and getting plenty of flying. This is what I wanted to do more than commanding others or flying a desk. I'm not very ambitious.

CHAPTER 19 - Exercise Golden Eagle

Volunteering to instruct VIPs involved me in a rather peculiar and unique adventure. A couple of days after having completed the Queen's Birthday fly past, the Chief Flying Instructor called me in his office to tell me that AOC 1 Group had selected me to fly Prince Charles as my co-pilot. Gulp! He added that if it had been left to him, he would do the flight himself (of course). However, he had no choice as the AOC had chosen me. Prince Charles was training on the Jet Provost at RAF Cranwell in July 1971 and the RAF thought that he should have an idea of front-line work by flying in a Phantom, a Nimrod and a Vulcan. A detailed plan was produced, Exercise Golden Eagle.

The prince flew in the back seat of the Phantom in a practice interception and some general handling (the back seat is the navigator's station and has no flying controls). The Nimrod flight included a longish transit to the operating area, low-level search over the sea then a transit back to base. In the Vulcan he was to fly as the co-pilot. The flight was to consist of the type of training sortie a front-line crew would fly. I planned to climb to high level, carry out a handling demonstration and let HRH practise, followed by a descent to low level (500 feet above the terrain) along the east coast, then a simulated low-level bombing attack and return to base for a few circuits and a final landing using the tail brake parachute.

The total arrangement for Golden Eagle was hybrid. The crew was from 44 squadron, headed by Flt Lt Pete Perry, based at Waddington. Two aircraft were to be supplied by RAF

Scampton. I was the captain for the event, flying from RAF Waddington. Pete would fly in the 6th (passenger) seat able to operate switches on the starboard console normally the responsibility of the co-pilot. Pete would also serve the in-flight meals and drinks on a silver salver! [19]

This combination of crews, aircraft and operating base was complicated and although the chief reason for the flight from Waddington was that Prince Charles at Cranwell would not have to drive through busy Lincoln.

The order stipulated that all safety modification were to be incorporated and, and as much fatigue life as possible left on the aircraft. I arranged a meeting with the engineers. A list was produced of suitable aircraft, from which I was to choose. Both engine types were represented, 200 and 300 series. Even if aircraft look the same, they don't always behave the same[20]. The two Vulcans I chose; I knew were reliable and very well behaved. They flew straight! They both had 200 series engines which I preferred because throttle response was so much quicker than the 300 series. Although the 300 series were more powerful, we used them in a derated configuration producing much the same thrust as the 200s. The choice was made, our two aircraft were: primary XL320 and XL392 as spare. A full air

---

[19] Andrew Brookes who was a flight commander on 44 squadron wrote a number of books about defence. In two of them he mentions this royal flight. In both he said Pete Perry was the captain. When I found out I was upset that my tiny bit of making history was being highjacked. I wrote to Brookes asking him to correct his mistakes but got no response. He is a military historian, a Fellow of the Royal United Services Institute.
[20] I give an example of different handling of the same make of aircraft in the chapter when I was an examiner.

test of each aircraft was required according to the order. Both air tests ended using the tail brake parachute.

During the air test of XL320, the retractable console between the two ejection seats had been stowed. The co-pilot pulled on the handle to move the console upright to do a fuel check. The handle came off in his hand as the console reached full travel. The handle was T-shape, like an old fashion hand brake handle which one pulled back from a car's dashboard. I handed it to the AEO to put in his desk drawer.

The brake chute provides superb deceleration. The AEO, so as not to forget the handle, had put it on the desk (it would have been hard to forget as there was no way the pilots could leave their seat with the fuel console upright). The rear crew desk, or work table, had a small raised border by some 3 or 4 millimetres to stop things like pencils from falling off the edge. As we decelerated when the chute bit, the handle slid forward (rear crew faced aft), hit the edge of the table and flew over the AEO's shoulder never to be seen again. Many man-hours were spent looking everywhere including pulling off some cabin wall insulation. I thought it might have landed in the open in-flight-meals metal box. This had been returned to the aircrew meal centre and, in turn, had been emptied and the contents with all the other meal centre rubbish had been taken to the tip. The tip was searched. The handle was not found. All this fuss of course was because it was unwise to have a potential loose article in the cabin carrying the heir to the throne. In the event, our primary aircraft became XL392 which was not as good an aircraft to fly but entirely satisfactory.

Much of Exercise Golden Eagle order had stipulated names, aircraft state, operating airfields and the length of the sortie. The trip itself was left to me. I tried to duplicate a normal squadron training sortie but with opportunities for minor demonstrations of aircraft handling and of course tried to give the prince as much handling as possible. Pete Perry's navigators and I drew up a route which we flew mainly for timing and practice purposes on 29th June. It worked out very well indeed and I informed AOC No. 1 Group of its suitability. The route was approved.

We carried out a number of rehearsals running up to the day. After each we would debrief in the aircrew meal centre discussing details and possible improvements. We normally sat in a group around a table close to the entrance door. During one of the debriefs, the door burst open and Squadron Leader Operations[21] (an old enemy of mine) shouted in a voice loud enough "Who chose 200 series engines for the royal flight". "I did, Sir" I replied "LeBrun, you're a F***ing idiot. Don't you know that 300 series engines can handle bird strikes much

---

[21] Squadron Leader John S. had been a Vulcan examiner. Everyone walked and flew in fear of him. He was a bully and being in a position of professional authority could make life very difficult for pilots and crew, and he did. In Goose Bay once he reported a failure that no one could decipher because of the wording that he had used. It turned out that an artificial feel unit had failed. For some time, I had been puzzled by the way the autopilot disengaged during the descent to low altitudes from 40,000 feet. In speed-lock mode, it would always kick out at about 25,000 feet. It disengaged causing the aircraft to rear upwards noticeably. I asked him what he thought the reason would be. After all he was a standardiser and knew all the answers. Of this question he did not know the answer but to cover his ignorance, he said, "Work it out for yourself, Boy!" I did not like the reply nor particularly being called "Boy". But kept my own counsel. I worked out the answer eventually and told him that I had, adding "I doubt that you did know, Sir, and we'll leave it at that".

better?" (There was a marginal statistical difference between the two series of engines). I said nothing and he departed. Of course, all the crews in the meal centre heard that outburst. I was quite upset.

The Station Commander at Waddington had been my student on the OCU and had taken over the station just a few weeks before Golden Eagle. He had told me that it all had to go well and that if I had any problems with anything on the station, I was to tell him right away. After being called a F***ing Idiot, I walked down to his office at the end of the corridor, told his PA that I had a problem with Golden Eagle and needed to see the Group Captain. I was shown in to his office right away, told him the story. "Come with me", he said. Off we went to the Operations Room where Sqn Ldr Ops worked, I was told to wait just outside. The door was left open and I heard the Station Commander say to John S. "Right John, you are off on leave for 10 days. Go now!" And he went. That was the only snag I had in Waddington. It was dealt with masterfully.

The last rehearsal took place on the 23 July 1971 with AVM Horsley, AOC Number 1 Group, acting as Prince Charles. The weather was good and we did everything we set out to do. The AVM gave his full approval with pleasure. It's interesting that during the high-level portion of the sortie, Air Traffic Control reminded us that this area would not be available in a few days as it was because of a royal flight. My reply simply, "Roger, that will be us". No reply from the controller.

After this rehearsal, AVM Horsley gave me a personal briefing. "You will be flying with the heir to the throne and therefore, if anything happens to the aircraft forcing an abandonment, he is to go first." I acknowledged that I understood. I had my own thoughts on this matter, and I left it as that.

On Monday 26th July, eve of the Golden Eagle flight, I had arranged that Prince Charles should have an hour or so in the Vulcan simulator in Waddington. That would give him some familiarity with the flight deck, strapping in procedures, etc. It also gave me the chance to give him a full safety briefing. He seemed particularly interested and quite keen to handle the simulator. But although the stick forces in the simulator were realistic, I told him the aircraft was very pleasurable and not difficult to handle.

A cocktail party had been arranged for that Monday evening with Prince Charles. Lots of new hats, frocks and shoes and for the chaps, clean, sombre lounge suits. The party went well. Those that were to participate in the flight were off to bed early. Our take-off time was 1000 hours. The whole crew including HRH arrived at about 0700 hours. It was also our wedding anniversary. I could have had enough on my plate to forget it, but I didn't. There was a big kiss for Carole, an anniversary card and a bit of a present all handed over at 6.30 am.

L to R Pete Marsland (plot.), Gordon Heath (rad.), HRH, Ian Washington (AEO), Pete Perry (6th seat/waiter) Author (captain).

The weather was superb but the forecast for the east coast low-level route was poor with low clouds obscuring the ground from the Firth of Forth all the way to Flamborough head. It looked like that part of the trip would be flown at safety altitude, well above the cloud tops. Still. it was an opportunity for the co-pilot to handle the aircraft much more than if we had been at low-level. We had a royal pre-flight breakfast, changed into our clean and tidy flying clothing and off to XL392 which was parked quite close to the Operations Block. Already there was a crowd of Number 1 Group, Waddington and Scampton senior staff to see us off. A few photos were taken. Subsequently, I found out that Pete Perry made sure that the prince and his crew were photographed together with me on one side (above). This made cropping the photo much easier, cutting me out altogether.

The aircraft behaved impeccably. We took off exactly on time, climbed to our normal cruising altitude (no problems with Air Traffic Control, the way ahead was clear). A few minutes after take-off, giving my co-pilot time to take a deep breath, I handed him control to maintain 250 knots. He did that impeccably at the same time as keeping a good lookout – not easy to do in a Vulcan, but he still detected aircraft a long way away as tiny dots which I could not see. At 20,000 feet I asked him to lower the nose a bit and let the speed increase to 300 knots. No problems there at all so I let him transfer to 0.86 IMN and level off at about FL410. We did the top-of-climb checks while Pete Perry did a fuel check. I demonstrated a few characteristics of the Vulcan but mainly let him handle the aircraft. He did that well and confidently. We did a high-level simulated attack on a Scottish target which, as I have mentioned before is not very exciting for the front end. After this, I spent some time explaining the various lever, dials and switches: their use and functions. That took some time – there are lots of these on the Vulcan flight deck.

We were soon over northern Scotland where we turned round in preparation for our descent to low level. Just as forecast, low cloud covered the route but we were in the clear flying at safety altitude. Nevertheless, we did a simulated attack on some imaginary target off Flamborough Head then set heading for Waddington. Once in the circuit we carried out a few instrument approaches and overshoots using the ILS (with which he was familiar) then a very accurate internal aids approach from which we rolled into the visual circuit. I let Prince Charles fly much of the instrument approaches taking over just a mile or so before touch down. He soon got the idea of using a boot-full of rudder on initiating turns. But the visual circuits were mine with one roller then the final landing with the brake 'chute, after precisely 3 hours in the air. It all went like clockwork. We climbed out of the aircraft and he was whipped off to Cranwell after shaking hands with everyone and thanking us.

It was over. All the excitement and effort had paid off. The AOC thanked us all and we went home. There was a get together that evening in Waddington where a few beers were consumed. Back to work the following day, Wednesday, I ferried an aircraft from a Rolls-Royce worksite, Bitteswell in Nottinghamshire, where Olympus engines were serviced and modified. On Thursday, I carried out a final handling test of a co-pilot on his left-hand seat conversion course. Carole was on school summer break so we took the whole of August to caravan in France. Later that year, we all received a Christmas card signed 'Charles'.

****

At the OCU, most if not all the QFIs carried out Vulcan flying displays. Mr Vulcan, Squadron Leader Joe L'Estrange had developed a superb display pattern that everyone copied. Joe in fact checked most of us for the display. The display took 6 minutes and the aircraft was never more than a mile from the display centre (centre of the front of the crowd), and although it required some skill, it was very safe yet showed the Vulcan qualities well. If the display was from take-off, once the undercarriage was up, a steep, full-power climb and turn was initiated to 1,500 feet at about 190 knots some 30 to 40 degrees off the runway heading. At the top of the climb, a turn back and a descent to 250 feet above the runway was started. The aircraft rolled out on the runway heading at the right height flying at less than 200 knots. Opposite the centre of the display, a 360 degrees turn was carried out with the aircraft clean (U/C up, airbrakes in and bomb doors closed). Rolling out of the turn, again full power was applied (the crowd loved the noise) and a repeat manoeuvre at the other end of the airfield was carried out aiming once more to be on height and runway heading at the finish. Another 360-degree turn was initiated but this time with the U/C down, airbrakes out and bomb doors open. On the roll out the aircraft was cleaned up, full power applied for a very steep climb spraying the crowd with much noise. Very occasionally when we needed to land at the display airfield, we still climbed steeply and held off for other displays to take place. Eventually we'd land using the brake parachute. From 1969 until the end of my tour, I did a substantial number of displays without running into any problems. One of the advantages of the L'Estrange display was that there were equivalent to exit doors throughout the flight. I remember that on one display at RAF Leeming, I had not reached 1,500 feet above ground as I turned back towards the airfield. Rather than keep the turn and the descent going, which could end in disaster, I decided half way down to reverse the turn and complete a 270 degree turn onto the airfield in complete safety. I phoned the senior air traffic controller at the airfield after landing to ask if anything in my display looked wrong. "Far from it, it was wonderful". Good old Joe L'Estrange. He'd worked everything out carefully.

CHAPTER 20 - Cyprus

In October 1971 I received a signal that I was posted to Cyprus as Officer Commanding the Vulcan Flight Simulator. A ground tour was something I was trying to avoid like. I phoned a friend who just happened to be the PA to my old student, AVM Horsley, AOC Number 1 Group. I asked him if there was any way my posting could be changed to a slot on 35 or 9 Squadrons both based in Akrotiri, Cyprus. I'll ask, he said. He phoned back soon after. My posting could not be changed. In any case, this was to Cyprus: duty-free booze, cigarettes, cars; cheap restaurant meals; wonderful scenery; but most of all, summer nearly all year round (not quite, as we found out) with beach clubs, and a superb social life. I had to accept the decision, but the Chief Flying Instructor bollocked me for going directly to the AOC. I should not have done that. But I explained that I only talked to an officer of equal rank to mine. Surely nothing wrong with that surely.

Carole was delighted. Imagine, all that sun, warm sea, exotic food (sort of). She was very pleased indeed. Daughter Michelle was 3 years old and would probably start some form of schooling in Cyprus.

My new job was starting in January 1972 and I would be given 10 days overlap with the current boss of the simulator to learn the tricks of the trade. I was also told that unlike the UK simulators, OC simulator at Akrotiri was in charge of all three simulators technical personnel and the instructional support, two Master Pilots. I was also to be responsible for the navigators and the AEO simulators, but not their instructors, one of whom in any case outranked me.

I talked the boss and Number 1 Group to let me have a Lone Ranger to Akrotiri. This was readily agreed, particularly that the rear crew were recent ex-Vulcan on ground jobs in No 1 Group HQ in Bawtry. My co-pilot was also on a ground job at RAF Finningley running the simulator there.

The Vulcan bomb bay was huge. On Rangers we carried spares in a pannier hoisted on the bomb racks. The space in the pannier was normally taken up (mostly) by aircraft spares. But because Akrotiri housed 2 Vulcan Squadrons we did not need much space in it for spares. Instead, we carried a lot of the goods I were planning to take to Cyprus, including, of all things, a tumble dryer! (At the end of my tour, we left the dryer in Cyprus). An old mate from 617 Squadron, Eddie Baker, now on 35 Squadron, offered to store my goods until we arrived in January. I also heard that motor dealers in Cyprus were very keen to buy second hand British registered cars in part exchange. At the time, we drove a 1966 Riley 4/72 with about 45,000 miles, some of which towing a caravan, but in very good condition all round. I had taken a couple of photos of the car to take with me.

We departed from Scampton on Friday 19th November in XH559 arriving in Akrotiri just 4 hours and 15 minutes later. Once the aircraft was put to bed for the weekend and the panier emptied into a van that Eddy had managed to get from the RAF MT section in Akrotiri. The contents were put into 35 Squadron store. After a shower we shot off to Limassol for our evening meal. I was very busy the following day, going from one car dealer to another looking at new cars and offering the Riley as part exchange. One dealer, Volvos and Datsuns, offered £600 unseen, against the purchase of a Volvo P144 and a Datsun Cherry. These amounted to £1,800 leaving just £1,200 left to pay. What a fantastic offer. In the UK those cars would cost nearly double and I certainly would not get £600 for the Riley. The decision was made, we would drive to Cyprus. Absolutely mad!

****

We started in the first days of 1972 after the Christmas and New Year celebrations at Carole's parents were over. We had found tenants for our bungalow in North Hykeham near Lincoln. The tenant was an RAF colleague whose crew was involved in the royal flight. The premises were fully furnished.

Just beyond London, the fan belt broke in pouring rain. Fortunately, we were members of the AA and although we were a little delayed at Dover, the repair was done on the roadside. (This in the days where minor engine repairs were easily done, unlike today).

Michelle was very good. She sat on the back seat and did not complain at all although there was plenty for her to complain about with so much travelling. We had a cassette tape of Under Milkwood, which she listened to constantly whenever she got bored. I am afraid my timing for our first night stop was poor. We ended up sleeping in the car some distance south of

Frankfurt.

The following day the weather was good. We crossed the Alps through the tunnel into Austria then Yugoslavia. This time we were determined to get a good night's sleep so we stopped at a small hotel on the roadside in Yugoslavia. It was very spartan. The meal was not much either, neither was the breakfast. We were in another world. I had been briefed not to take any RAF uniforms or pieces that could identify me as military. I had retained my Canadian passport, which did not indicate my occupation. Still, from Zagreb eastward and southward we were followed all the way to the Greek border. Once we had left the Slovenian or European part of Yugoslavia into the Balkans proper, it became obvious that this was a poor, not very attractive country. We stopped in Skopje for refuelling where young boys were quite aggressive in asking for "Dinaries", the local currency. Soon we crossed in to Greece and stopped at the first hotel we saw. This Epiphany, the 6th of January. Another reason for Greeks to celebrate and of course there was a party at the hotel with a small band and many people enjoying themselves. The hotel was no more than a mile from the Yugoslav border. After the party, in our room, we could hear the barking of dogs patrolling the no-man's-land between the two countries.

The following day we drove to Athens. We had a few days before taking the ferry for Limassol at Piraeus. We visited the Acropolis, drove down to the Corinth canal, as well as to the ruins of Delphi on the Peloponnese. Greeks, like most Mediterranean people are very fond of children. We had

131

stopped at a restaurant for lunch on the terrace outside. After the meal, the proprietor just picked an orange from a tree and offered it to Michelle. She was fascinated to see oranges hanging from trees. I remember well how she broke into a wonderful, surprised smile when she was offered one.

A Greek company ran the ferry, of course. In the previous years, some disasters had befallen Greek shipping and the rules had been tightened. Every day on the poop deck, the crew assembled and were briefed by the captain. The written safety instructions were clear. If the ship's siren sounded for more than some 30 seconds, passengers were to leave their cabin and assemble on deck wearing their life-saving jackets. We had an inside cabin which was very hot. As the ship sailed through narrows between islands, the siren started to sound continuously. We were awake because of the heat. We rushed on deck not having found our life jackets. Although the siren was still sounding, everything appeared normal. The ship was smoothly sailing by the islands. It must have been around midnight and the islanders certainly could not sleep with this racket going on. In the morning, we arrived at Rhodes for a few hours. I was amazed at the way the ship was docked. The whole vessel was being pulled onto the side of the dock by its own cables and winches. A cable snap could whip off heads. Later on that day, we arrived in Limassol. There were no docks there. The ship unloaded, including our car, using lighters. But the sea was calm and lighters came alongside without problems. The car was driven on. We had arrived at last in Cyprus for a wonderful three years.

Our good friends, Eddy and Ginty Baker, put us up until we found accommodation. We slept well that first night. Michelle got up early and went onto the terrace in the warm sunshine. She fell asleep there. We found her curled up with her panda bear, Chi-chi, a short while later. She was a picture of rest and peace. I will never forget that scene.

Over the next couple of days, we were shown the ropes by Eddy and Ginty. Although the RAF provided accommodation, there was a queue to get a flat or a house. Until our turn came, which could take a few weeks, we had to find our own accommodation. This was not difficult. There was already a system of estate agents who literally fought to get clients.

****

In Cyprus, girls are given a dowry by their parents when they marry. Because the RAF and the army had such a large number of personnel, dowry houses, and flats were there for the choosing of prospective tenants. We found a brand-new ground floor furnished flat just off the Limassol bypass. Although there was no electricity yet, the estate agent installed an extension from a Cypriot neighbour to power us at least for a day or two. It was not cold but we needed some heating at night. We bought a gas heater (it was still in working condition 40 years later as we gave it to a charity) as well as a few items that we either had forgotten or did not have. The system in Limassol worked in a way that an estate agent who got your custom, would automatically get a percentage commission for all the household goods that were bought by his client. No wonder they were keen to get us on their book.

After a couple of months, we were asked to see a house in Ayios Athasnasios, just a short distance from the Limassol bypass. If satisfactory, this accommodation, a first floor flat, would be taken over by the RAF as an official hiring. I do not know how much the landlord charged the RAF, but we paid the RAF-set rent. The flat was delightful with large airy rooms, and a balcony overlooking Limassol, Limassol Bay, and Akrotiri, which is Greek for peninsula. There was a small café run by Peter. He had spent 14 years in Australia. His wife made wonderful Greek sandwiches and his coffee was strong. He also sold beer and wine as well as locally produced brandy and such like. He spoke English with an accent that was an odd mixture of Greek overlaid by Australian. We got used to it eventually. There was also diagonally opposite us an open-air cinema with very loud music. Fortunately, it showed films only once per week.

Carole did not work initially but we knew that there were posts in local service-run schools for qualified teachers. Our social life was very lively. We dined out frequently. We were invited by Cypriot neighbours and friends to weddings, christening, or just a religious feast. Having the first RAF hiring in the village we were a curiosity to the locals. They were kind and Michelle was much admired for her black hair and fair skin.

For Greek Orthodox, Easter is the most important religious holiday of the year. We were invited to an ox roast. We mixed readily with the local population. We spoke no Greek and few of them spoke English. We always managed to communicate nevertheless. One villager who spoke some English asked us what the British did at religious holidays. We pointed out that Christmas was more important because it was a family occasion when we exchanged presents and had a family meal. "What do you eat?" he asked. "Usually, a turkey stuffed with all kinds of goodies". "Ah", he said", you will not eat turkey here. There is only one turkey in the village and he is now Christian".

CHAPTER 21 - The Flight Simulator

My new job as Officer Commanding the Vulcan Flight Simulator and Trainers (there was a navigators' trainer and a combined electrics and electronics trainer for AEOs) as I indicated previously, included responsibility for all the technical personnel from Junior Technician to Flight Sergeant and Master Aircrew. The three trainers were housed in the same air-conditioned building within the area reserved for Bomber Wing. The Wing was headed by a Wing Commander assisted by two specialist officers, a Pilot and a Navigator or AEO. The simulator was my direct responsibility, while a navigator and an AEO, although part of the staff, were autonomous, and ran the other two trainers. There were 13 technicians to look after the simulator and trainers. There was also another pilot as simulator instructor and two simulator assistants, Master Pilots (a rank equivalent to Warrant Officer 1st Class).

I took over in mid-February 1972 after a hand over of a few days with my predecessor. It became obvious that he had left the whole unit in a barely adequate state. The technicians were are very competent and well led by a Flight Sergeant but their skills and the leadership provided were not appreciated. I think this was chiefly because the man in charge did not care much for the job in hand. There seem to be some form of acceptance by Bomber Wing, that this was the best that could be done. I'll explain:

Each crew needed a minimum of 3 hours of flight simulator and an equivalent of navigation and electronic training every month, were not made to work hard in the flight simulator sometimes not at all. During the 3 hours slot, they did not spend more than one hour in the flight simulator (aka The Box). Fortunately, both the navigator and AEO trainers were more professional and real-value training was given there. Irrespective of what they did, captains and co-pilots were logged for 3 hours training which would show on their squadron training board and in their individual logbooks.

Prior to my arrival, time spent in the simulator was so unrealistic that often crews would come out of the machine sweating and sometime swearing having been put through a number of emergencies that were improbable. This behaviour by the instructors insured that crews detested the simulator.

It is generally understood, that aircrew are trained to deal with one major emergency. Failures of other systems, a cascade resulting from the initial problem were part of the same emergency. The principle is that crews with a major difficulty in flight should be trained to deal with that problem and return to the earth safely. If other major problems emerge, the emergency could easily turn into a disaster. If it did and the crew manages to deal with it, it was sometimes worth a decoration in recognition,

My predecessors in the simulator made life difficult if not impossible for crews. I witnessed a number of crews dealing well with an emergency, being given yet another major failure entirely divorced from the original problem. This was anathema to me. In psychology, it is called aversive conditioning which means "this is a punishment, so do not do it again". That is exactly the way crews felt about the simulator. Something had to be done. The handover was complete and I was now responsible for crew training as well as for the simulator staff. Over a few weeks, I designed a set of exercises for the crews. I consulted the navigator and electronic trainer instructors, who also were new to the job, to ensure that at least we were trying to achieve much the same thing. Vulcan crews in Cyprus have a tour of 30 months. With leave and other activities, this meant some 24-simulator slots. I designed 24 exercises ranging from relatively easy to more difficult but never breaking the rule of no more than one major failure, except in one exercise, where the problems were such that the crew had to bail out. Not all crews judged it right and some crews "perished".

Turkey, Cyprus's northern neighbour was part of NATO as well as in the Central Treaty Organisation (CENTO) as was then Iran. Crews occasionally had to fly to various military airfields in both Turkey and Iran. Sometimes these were official visits or just liaison. Familiarisation with Turkish and Iranian routes and destination airfields would be done in the simulator. I even tried to put on various accents pretending to be an air traffic controller. I gave erroneous air traffic information to the crew, creating a clash of route or altitude with another aircraft. Not all crews detected this. In the following debrief I brought that error up. I do not believe there was ever such a real error by air traffickers but at least it made the crews aware and maybe smile a little.

Akrotiri Flight Simulator with instructors and technical personnel

In the spring, our family joined one of the beach clubs, the Water Ski Club. It was just that. Not everyone water-skied, but there were good facilities at the club where one could eat and drink for a fair price. From April on, work stopped at 1pm, giving a whole afternoon of relaxation. Carole also joined the Saddle Club and soon was involved in its running as well as riding frequently. But this was hot work and a quick trip to the beach club to refresh was always welcome. Michelle had not started school. She was four years old and very keen to be in the water. We had driven once to the north side of Cyprus going through a number of isolated Greek and Turkish villages. Indeed, if you were a Greek Cypriot, you would not be welcome at all in a

139

Turkish village and vice versa. Sometimes we would stop for a light refreshment. We were always shown how cruel either the Greeks or the Turks had been to the other side during the war of independence. There were always a number of photographs on a wall somewhere showing victims of the other side.

Eventually we would reach a small scalloped-shaped beach. Usually, we would be the only ones there. The sea even early in the swimming season would be warm and very warm by September or October. We had either a picnic that Carole had prepared or light a barbecue and cook some meat. Although it took well over an hour to reach this beach, it was worth every minute of the trip.

****

The Wing Commander in charge of Bomber Wing was Wing Commander Tiny (he was not) M. The pilot specialist to whom I reported was an old mate from the OCU, Joe L'Estrange. When we arrived in Akrotiri, Joe was in the last month of his tour. He briefed me that Tiny M. was a very odd person indeed. "If you recommend something, he will take the exact opposite view and decide on that." I could not believe that he behaved as such. Any recommendation had to be 180 degrees from what was required?

I had a secondary duty. I was in charge of flight safety for Bomber Wing as well as security of the bomber area in case of tension. Once Tiny asked me to get sandbags to protect the Bomber Wing and Squadron buildings. I thought it a good idea and I contacted the chap in charge of the RAF Regiment with the request. "No can do!" was the reply. I can't remember why that was. I relayed this to the Boss. "Alright then," he said, "there are lots of cement factories on this island, get cement bags instead". The laugh I got from the RAF Regiment could be heard in Limassol, 10 miles away. "Problem is, old boy, when the cement gets wet, and it will, it hardens and bullets hitting it produce some perfectly good shrapnel. Tell your boss". I did. He was not pleased and held it against me for the rest of his tour, which, as it turned out was cut short. More of that later.

****

In June 1972, I received a phone call from the station Commander, my old student Air Commodore David Craig. He congratulated me on receiving the Air Force Cross. I was flabbergasted. AOC No 1 Group (also an ex-student), my previous unit, 230 OCU, RAF Scampton, and even my old squadron boss all sent me signals and letters congratulating me. It was awarded for services rendered and not for bravery (just as well). This is the citation:

Flight Lieutenant LeBrun is a French-Canadian who joined the RAF in 1961 after serving with the RCAF for several years during which time he became an experienced flying instructor on Harvards. After tours as co-pilot on Number 83 Squadron and as a captain on Number 617 Squadron, he came to Number 230 Operational Conversion Unit on 29 July 1968 as a flying instructor.

He worked extremely hard and set himself the highest of standards. He was not happy with his performance unless it was as near perfect as possible. He always takes every opportunity to fly and has to date competed 2100 hours on Vulcan aircraft. In May 1970, he upgraded his category to A2 and by his precept and example encouraged other instructors to study and improve their own categories. He has a zest for flying and hard work, which endears him to both staff and students alike. In October 1970, he was made an Instrument Rating Examiner, and because of his boundless natural ability, he was given an Exceptional assessment as pilot in 1971.

He has been the natural selection on the Unit to instruct Senior Officers and because his temperament and success in this direction he had the honour to fly with His Royal Highness the Prince of Wales in a Vulcan during July 1971. For the past two years, he has flown in the Vulcan aircraft, which led the Strike Command formation that flew over Buckingham Palace on Her Majesty the Queen's Birthday Celebration Flypasts. Furthermore, he has acted as the Unit display pilot on several occasions and as a result of his immaculate performances, laudatory letters have been received praising his excellent timing and technique.

This fine instructor has been of incalculable value to his Unit and to the Vulcan Force. By his splendid example, he has raised the standards of flying within the unit by helping and encouraging less gifted students to achieve more than satisfactory results thus enabling them to go to their Squadrons with the personal drive for improvement, which is so necessary. The continued high quality of his work and his devotion to the task are deserving of recognition, and it is therefore recommended that he be awarded the Air Force Cross on the occasion of Her Majesty the Queen's Birthday

Honours."

Air Force Cross

Of course, all this is well over the top. I do not think that I was that good and I have a feeling that the AFC was awarded as an alternative to promotion. With the proviso mentioned above, I would have liked promotion, but of concern, was the possibility of just one flying tour in rank. In any case, I thought I would never be fit for further promotion.

Air Force Cross presentation - HQ NEAF, Episkopi, Cyprus - 1972

The presentation took place in Cyprus by Air Marshal Sir Derek Hodgkingson rather than by the Queen.

Carole and Michelle were not present, as Carole had managed to get a place on an RAF flight to the UK. These flight opportunities were rare occurrences and not to be missed.

CHAPTER 22 - CENTO

In 1972 and 1973, the RAF organised a major exercise with the Iranian Air Force (IAF). Base in Teheran as part of a CENTO exercise. I volunteered to be the admin and general dogsbody officer. I flew there in the back of a C130 Hercules, it was noisy and slow. Four Vulcans were participating in the exercise that consisted of low-level interceptions with Iranian Air Force fighters. We landed in 40C temperatures in Mehrabad, Teheran's main airport at an altitude of about 4,000 feet above sea level. The maddest driver I have ever encountered took us in a mini-bus to a hotel in Teheran. Allah was working very hard to protect us from accidents in the furious city traffic.

My job was to organise in-flight rations for the crews, supervise the security of ground equipment and when any Vulcan was airborne, be the duty and liaison pilot in the control tower. All the Iranians I met were very kind, interesting, interested, and co-operative. The chef who prepared the in-flight meals was Swiss and had spent a lot of time in the UK. He was surprised and pleased when I addressed him in French and we got on very well. The arrangement was to pick up the meals at about 9am in a refrigerated van. The security police inspected them before loading in the van. The chef always had a full English breakfast ready for both of us when I arrived. We'd spent 30 or 40 minutes just shooting the breeze. We were always accompanied by an Iranian Air Force officer wherever we went on duty. On one occasion walking through the main passenger terminal in uniform, this young lieutenant reached over and held my hand. Oh dear! I thought, what do I do now?

145

All I could think was to change my briefcase from the other hand to that one. He promptly moved to my other side. Unbeknown to me, some of the Vulcan crews were on the mezzanine above the main concourse having a good laugh at my discomfiture. I subsequently found out that holding hands with other men was a normal thing in Iran

The man in charge of Mehrabad's airfield lighting was British, Mike Cherry, who had been in Teheran for some years. I met him in the passenger terminal and he invited me for a meal with his family at his house that very evening. He and his wife just wanted to speak English. They were homesick and although very well paid, neither he nor his wife was happy in Iran. We had a good meal and a very good chat too. I'd noticed in Teheran at the entrance of many houses, a large cube fixed to the wall over the door. It turned out to be the cheapest air conditioning system there is. The cube is about 1 metre per side. It contains a circular water-filled trough in which a fibre wick stands. Above this arrangement, there is a fan and from the cube, a flue passes inside the house. It works on water evaporation. Its efficiency is extraordinary. I said to my host that I did not think the system could be that good. It was hot in the house, well over 30C. He turned on the fan, and within five minutes, I asked him to turn it off; I was cold. The only power the system uses is a low wattage fan, and water, which refills the trough automatically as it, evaporates. Very, very impressive.

Teheran, other than being mad with traffic, was an interesting city. I visited the main museum and saw the Peacock Throne as well as some delicate and delightful jewellery, much of it made of turquoise, a locally mined semi-precious gem. As you would expect, the Suk was a jumble of alleyways with shops selling Iranian carpets, copper dishes, plates or various sizes and vases. Some carpets were absolutely beautiful, and expensive even by Western standards. It was good fun to get the price down: indeed, it was expected. I bought some jewellery for Carole as well as a copper plate. We still have some rings that I bought during that visit.

We flew back to Akrotiri after a few days. The following year I did not volunteer to go. On that detachment, one of the Vulcans in Mehrabad suffered a major hydraulic failure and could not lower one of its undercarriage main legs, even using the emergency system. The landing was well handled by Eddy Baker and everyone got out without a scratch. Our Bomber Wing senior engineer was very annoyed that he had not been consulted while the aircraft was still airborne. He had been a Vulcan crew chief for many years prior to being commissioned. He had always worked on Vulcans. There was nothing that man did not know about the airframe, its engines, and the multiplicity of systems. When he was told of the problem, the first thing he said was "Have they tried the emergency hydraulic pack?" It had not been tried. When the fault was duplicated with an aircraft on jacks, what he had suggested worked. Too bad when the accident happened, he was in Akrotiri and the aircraft was in Teheran. Still, a quick telephone call from Iran could have saved one Vulcan and a somewhat shaken crew.

After a few months in Cyprus, Carole obtained a post at the Berengaria primary school near Limassol. Although British

147

Services employed her, she was paid and considered to be a local employee. This meant an income tax of two and one half per cent, and a bonus at the end of the year of a thirteenth month salary. It did not take long at that rate to pay off our mortgage of £11 a month for the bungalow in Lincolnshire. At the same time, house prices in the UK were inflating at an amazing rate. We were glad of our decision not to sell. I had a colleague who sold his house in a village near Lincoln for £4,500. After his 3 years away, that house fetched £11,000. He could not afford to buy it back.

My work in the simulator was proceeding well. All of the trainers were electronically driven, they worked on analogue principles. There were very large cabinets in the flight simulator hall that contained electronic valves, banks of variable resistors, capacitors and so on. The navigator trainer had a very large map of an imaginary country (including airfields named Burgess and McClean) in the form of an enormous photographic negative in a dark cabinet, over which a camera moved in the appropriate direction and speed producing a radar-like picture on the H2S radar screen. The ECM and electric trainer was small by comparison but very complex and duplicated exactly the aircraft electrical and electronic counter measures systems.

I had been thinking how these three trainers could be joined to produce realistic war sortie training within the limits of the various simulators. I consulted my technicians and the rest of the work force. This was a professional challenge. They all gave the idea full support, indeed they were enthusiastic. I still had to convince OC Bomber wing - the one who always took the opposite decision to recommendations made. Fate came to my rescue.

Tiny M. captained a single Vulcan to an airfield in Iran on a liaison visit. In addition, the visit included practicing low-level over desert parts of the country. On his return I was asked, as Bomber Wing Flight Safety Officer, to prepare a special incident report (SOR) because the top of the aircraft wing appeared crinkled and there was excessive G registered on the fatigue counter. Tiny M. told me that this had happened at low level as he passed over a protruding hill on the flat terrain over which he was flying at some 350 knots. I started to fill in the SOR when the senior engineer phoned: "John don't fill the SOR just yet, there is other information that may change the reason for the damage". A few hours later it came out that our trusty leader had had a heavy night with the Iranian Air Force base commander, promising a flying display and high-speed pass when he departed the following morning. This was duly carried out and the Vulcan was badly damaged. M. was relieved of his post, got back to the UK, took his boat out in the Atlantic, and was never seen again.

His replacement, Wing Commander Alun Morgan was very different from his predecessor. I had known him as a flight commander on one of the Scampton squadrons. He was highly regarded, efficient and understanding. We got along famously from the very beginning.

Social life in Akrotiri was dynamic and good fun. Although we still lived some distance from base, we took part in nearly all social activities from formal dining-in nights and annual balls, to being with friends in the bar or in a Limassol restaurant. We were invited to a wedding in the town of Paphos, nearly the western-most point of the island. Cypriot weddings did not spare the food nor the dancing. We had gone with a Cypriot friend of Eddy and Jinty, Emilio. He owned a restaurant as well as being a police officer. Although his restaurant had not the best atmosphere in town, the food was always good as was the wine.

CHAPTER 23 - A Surprise Visit

One day, at work in the Cyprus flight simulator, I received a call from the station commander's P.A. "Prince Charles is stopping over shortly. He is on his way to Hong Kong. The stopover will be about 90 minutes. Could you look after him in the simulator for an hour or so?" Gulp! "The simulator is shut down on maintenance", I said. "When is he arriving?" "Actually, he's landed already and I thought of you because of your flight with him not long ago." said the P.A. "OK, bring him over but just give me a few minutes". I rushed out of my office into the simulator hall. "Please put the box back on line," I said. "We've got a VIP coming, Prince Charles". "Ah boss, always for the joke then". "This is no joke", I replied, "It's for real".

Normally it took between 30 and 40 minutes to get the simulator running. The lads did it in just a few minutes. They were very much open mouthed when HRH walked-in. I introduced them all. It made their day, but it gave me a few more grey hairs. When Alun Morgan learnt about this, he was very reproachful. I had not called him. I really had so little time and so much to do I just did not think of him. He did not hold it against me.

****

After some 18 months in Ayios Athanasios, a married quarter on camp became available. Quarters in Akrotiri were ex-ground-nut scheme from East Africa. They looked and felt like railway carriages. They were built of some type of plywood, which the termites adored. They munched away at the stuff leaving just the coat of paint behind. However, the maintenance people were used to that and a repair would be done pronto. There was a fireplace, which was very cosy on the very few cold nights in the winter. The kitchen was to one side and adequate for the purpose. Michelle had her own bedroom and of course, now that we were in quarters, her own friends close by. She was doing well at school and loved swimming at the ski club.

Carole was still deeply involved with the Saddle Club. She had been appointed treasurer. This was an impossible job. The club had a small bar and served light snacks.

The Akrotiri Saddle Club

There was no accounting and the barman was deep in with the suppliers. Although the club did not lose money, it made little considering the turnover. The other members of the management committee were volunteers like Carole, but the club was expected to be run along military accounting rules. The station commander inspected the premises from time to time just as he would squadron offices or the armoury. Horses are not tidy animals and although the two grooms were skilled, military cleanliness and discipline did not fit in at all with their idea of looking after horses.

Frequently, one of the British Regiments based on the island would use the club facilities. This is how an army officer of the Royal Anglian Regiment heard that Carole was a violinist. Would she be willing to play for the Tattoo in Happy Valley at the near-by RAF and Army headquarters, Episkopi?

The Tattoo did not take place every year. This was the first for some 3 or 4 years. The army was organising the show. The theme was the Highland Clearances. The army chap had chosen the second movement of Dvorak's New World symphony. It was said that the tune, normally played on the oboe, came from a Negro spiritual in the US. This was contended by the Scots who claimed that it came from the song Going Home. Whatever the source it is a beautiful tune.

That part of the Tattoo took place in Happy Valley, Episkopi, after dusk with Highlanders drifting by in the background while Carole, dressed as a male highlander, played her violin. It was very moving. The following evening, the Tattoo was repeated in the eastern part of the island. Carole was driven there and treated as a VIP (quite rightly) having been given the General Officer Commanding's bungalow and all the trimmings. It was a great success. A friend of ours did not believe Carole was the violinist. "It was a fellow", he kept repeating. To this day, he still does not believe us.

CHAPTER 24 - War Games

My plan to link the three trainers was being implemented. The technicians spent a lot of time solving the many problems that arose. Eventually we got the system adequately serviceable. After long and very productive meetings, we three instructors devised an exercise which we thought would replicate, as best we could, a sortie into enemy territory. The map, which we used in the flight simulator, was the same as the navigators' imaginary country. The electronics trainer was small and mobile so we moved it during these special exercises next to the navigators' work place. In fact, the three rear crew were sitting in positions similar to those in the aircraft.

After a few runs through with different crews, it was concluded that this was a valuable training aid. The navigation instructor, Maurice Webster was also responsible for updating real target material and ensuring the crews were fully aware of new information. He had a direct contact at the Headquarters of Near East Air Force in Episkopi, just down the road. The simulated sortie we had put together tried to replicate the sort of land and sea the crews would overfly in the real case. The departure airfield, like Akrotiri, was on an island some 40 miles from the mainland. As in the real case, crews were held waiting for the release message over the sea at various altitudes, none of which was very high. It dawned on us that a man in a rowboat with a few shoulder-launched ground-to-air missiles could easily bring down a clutch of Vulcans for little risk. This information was very well received in Episkopi, and the war plan changed from holding aircraft over the sea to moving them over land.

Only a small change but we thought a valuable one. There were also a few other changes that our exercises produced and these were duly implemented, such as turning off the navigation lights.

My old student, Air Vice Marshal Peter Horsley, who had been AOC No. 1 Group, came to visit us. He was now Air Marshal Sir Peter, Deputy Commander, Strike Command. He was well aware of the work we had done. Indeed, he mentioned that we caused quite a stir in Strike Command with our suggestions about war routing of crews. I was delighted that all this work had been well worth it. The real brain behind the technical integration was Chief Technician Malcolm Redhead. He was not only a skilled, knowledgeable, and likeable man, but also a very good manager and leader. I made sure he, and the rest of the technical team got their share of the glory. My boss, Alun Morgan could not have been happier with the work we were doing.

Other than Bomber Wing flight safety, I was also responsible for the bomber area security in the event of tension or war. We were tested once or twice a year when a station-wide exercise was called. Night-time was always the most vulnerable. One of the lads, Jess, would volunteer to climb one of the few trees in the area and stay there all night with a walky-talky handset to keep us up to date with any suspicious movement within the Bomber Wing area. The rest of the staff would man checkpoints and set up small patrols. In the time I was in Akrotiri, the Bomber Wing area was never successfully penetrated. Some Khurkas tried their best at night, but Jess would always detect them. We would pass on the information to the Station Security flight who would handle the intruders.

****

Life was good. The meals in restaurants were cheap and plentiful. The booze was cheap and plentiful too. My weight increased commensurately and I ended up at 16 stones (over 100 kilos). At my annual medical, the doc suggested strongly that I lose weight. I said I would if my blood pressure was outside the limits. I knew that my blood pressure had always been low and this time too it was 120/80.

Much slimmer John and slim Carole

Nevertheless, I decided that I was becoming gross and decided to do something about it. I did what most doctors propose to reduce weight; I ate less. I ate a lot less. I ate so little (and drank not much) that within 4 months I was down to less than 12 stones. Now I started to look gaunt and friends worried that I had some disease or other. But no, I lost those four stones in the correct manner and for the right reasons. I still enjoyed my food, but less of it.

In late 1973, the CIA started to operate U2 aircraft from Akrotiri. We were told that they were used to help clear the Suez Canal after the conflicts between Israel and some Arab states. The staff that maintained and flew the aircraft were all USAF personnel on secondment to the CIA. Some of those people joined the various beach clubs. We were told that they were to be made welcomed. Some incoming CIA personnel spoke fluent Greek and did not participate much in the social life of the station. None of us was particularly concerned about this.

Cyprus had always been bubbling over with friction between its Greek and Turkish ethnic groups. There were also violent disputes between Greeks with showrooms and shops being blown up. In the countryside, Turkish villages would not let Greek Cypriots in, and vice-versa. Tension was always near the surface. The British had signed the Treaty of Establishment together with Greece and Turkey, when giving the island its independence and setting up the Cyprus Republic. The British had retained two areas on the island the Western Sovereign Base Area (SBA) and the Eastern SBA. Each signatory to the treaty committed their country to come to the assistance of

Cyprus particularly in defending its borders against aggression, and in preventing the division of the island. The Cyprus government was not to seek an alliance with any other state.

CHAPTER 25 - The Coup and the Invasion

In June 1974, one Nikos Sampson attempted a coup to oust Archbishop Makarios from the presidency of Cyprus. Although the coup was supposed to be sponsored by the Greek Colonels, there seemed little doubt, either in Athens or in Cyprus that the CIA was up to its neck in it. After a few days the coup failed but Turkish forces invaded the Island to protect its ethnic population. Eventually this resulted in partition where Turkish Cyprus occupied some 40% of the Island although the Turkish Cypriot population was only 18% of the total. I have no doubt that the UK failed in its duty to stop the coup at its start, and eventually to stop the Turkish invasion. Greek troop-carrying aircraft overflew the Western SBA on their way to Nicosia. This should not have been allowed. Lighting aircraft of 56 squadron could and should have diverted or maybe shot down at least one Greek aircraft after due warning, to encourage the others to turn back. Most Cypriots and most British on the island were certain that CIA operatives had trained Sampson over the period that the U2 had been operating. The USA thought that Makarios was a "goddamn commie". This was yet another example of failure of a CIA plan. CIA failures are legion. (See "A Legacy of Ashes", by Tim Weiner)

The Turkish fleet set off and unlike what happened in the 1960s did not turn back when Turkish Cypriots were threatened by Greek Cypriots. The invasion started and the UK did nothing about it. The Treaty of Establishment was not much use. I believe that the UK did not move against either Greece or Turkey because those old enemies would have used Cyprus as the battleground with the UK pig-in-the-middle. Instead, all UK personnel were withdrawn to the SBAs, waiting for some form of solution.

Well before this trouble started, Carole had managed to get another indulgence flight to the UK. The flight departed on time, just a day or two before the troubles started. As the Turkish invasion got under way, the RAF, not wanting to see its nuclear bomber force affected decided to withdraw one squadron to the UK and the other to Malta. I went to Malta as the squadron's general dogsbody. I stayed there for about 10 days until it was decided to fly the squadron back to the UK. I begged a seat in an Argosy transport aircraft back to Cyprus. Carole was due back in a day or so and I would be there to welcome her.

Our house had been used as accommodation for some 24 civilians from a BBC relay station nearby. By the time I arrived, they had all gone back to their own places. Our house was spotless. There was a nice message from our uninvited guests. The only damage was a broken glass. I was surprised that RAF rented accommodation could be used that way. However, those that stayed in our house were very well behaved. When Carole heard the story, she could hardly believe it.

About a week later early in the morning, the gang of 24 reappeared. There was yet another emergency and British nationals were evacuated once more into the SBAs. This time, the leader of the BBC group said, "Go back to sleep. We know where everything is". They were a good bunch. They stayed with us for a few days. Because we could not go shopping, we were handed army emergency rations. They were boxes containing enough food for five persons for one day. All boxes contained good quality food, but some boxes were in greater demand because they had perhaps a special pudding or a tasty curry and so on. The army also distributed frozen legs of lamb, frozen pork, or beef. We ate well and our expenditure was minimal. The NAAFI on camp still had plenty of booze.

Following the evacuation of front-line aircraft, Akrotiri, which had been the biggest, most active RAF station became like a ghost town. Except for a Hercules squadron and a Search and Rescue helicopter flight, there was no other aircraft. Over the next two months, things went back to a semblance of normality but without personnel to enjoy and share the work, it became unattractive. The simulator and all its equipment were to be repatriated also. My staff was leaving in dribs and drabs. Carole and I did not leave until January '75, thereby completing a full tour. The Turkish invasion squashed my plan to regain currency on the Vulcan in my last 6 months in Akrotiri. I was planning to fly just a few trips with a squadron QFI to be signed up as current in my log book. That would have permitted me to claim that I was current on the Vulcan and could return to the OCU as an instructor while waiting for an RAF decision on my future. I note that there were two years in Cyprus when I did not fly: 1972 and 1974. Of course, half of '74 there were no Vulcans in Akrotiri. Numbers 9 and 35 Squadrons were now back in the UK.

That not having worked out, I was most unhappy about my next posting: an instructor at the 230 OCU flight simulator at

162

RAF Finningley. That was me put on "hold".

CHAPTER 26 - Back to the UK

I spent a year in the Finningley simulator getting more and more depressed waiting for the RAF's decision about my future. Just about every crew coming through the simulator was experienced leaving the majority of instructing for the co-pilot's benefit. That too was depressing but on the other hand, I was required to be at work only when needed. This meant a maximum of 4 hours a day. It gave me the opportunity for some DIY in our house near Lincoln.

I was keen to keep flying and because the RAF had not indicated what it would do with me, I had to decide whether to leave the service and get civilian licences, find a job in Airlines, or wait until the RAF decided. I waited. Just a few months before my 38th birthday I received an offer of service as Specialist Aircrew to age 55. Specialist Aircrew meant just that: I would have jobs either flying or directly associated with flying. The salary increase was considerable too, and promotion to Squadron Leader was more or less assured at some time. I accepted the offer, and soon after I was sent on a refresher course on the (hated) JPs at RAF Leeming. This was in spite of my protestation that I really did not need a refresher as I was going straight back to flying instruction on 230 OCU. That cut no ice with the authorities. Ex-ground tour aircrew MUST have a flying refresher course. No argument there.

The Leeming course was quite straight forward. We flew some formation trips, which I had not done for a long time, that included formation approach and landing. The leader was flying exceptionally smoothly which made the job so much easier but I never found it that easy. I stayed in the Officers' Mess during the week and home at weekends. The course was only 5 weeks long. I returned to 230 OCU In March 1976.

****

During its long life as a Mk1, Mk1A, Mk2 and a Mk2K, the Vulcan was operated by up to 10 units, 9 of which were front line. Operating bases were Finningley, Scampton, Waddington, Coningsby, Cottesmore and Akrotiri in Cyprus. Waddington from 1956 until 1984 continuously operated Vulcans. By 1984, this was half of the RAF's life. Yet we hear more of the Lancaster than we do of the Vulcan, the Victor or the Valiant. Of course, the Lancaster was instrumental in winning World War 2, and some 55,000 aircrew perished. But the Vulcan helped to win and keep the peace, (notwithstanding the dispute in the South Atlantic in 1982). Perhaps the idea of a bomber able to destroy whole cities with a single weapon is still too uncomfortable to accept in British minds. They prefer, just a few small explosions from conventional bombs rather than a great big one.

With up to 55 aircrew per squadron the throughput of the OCU, the sole training unit was, at times prodigious. However, when I returned in 1976, two of the squadrons had already moved on to different aircraft, numbers 12 and 83. Yet with still 8 years to go, it was obvious that the Vulcan was approaching the end of its service career. We just did not know when. Nevertheless, seven squadrons were operational in 1976 and, except for number 27 squadron, involved in maritime reconnaissance, all were declared to SACEUR as available for war. But there was a shortage of crews and the OCU had to form a few operational crews to make up the numbers. That meant involving the unit in NATO Tactical Evaluations, Command, Group and station exercises. After nearly 20 years of existence free from those bothersome tasks, OCU staff were now called in the middle of the night to return to base and prepare for simulated war. There was a lot of resentment.

CHAPTER 27 – Back on the OCU

I still very much found it a pleasure to fly this wonderful aircraft regularly. I did a standard course followed by another QFI conversion course. This added to a fair number of flying hours. I think the OCU was not very busy at the time, so it was an opportunity for the current QFIs to do their basic and more advanced instructing. I was more than willing to listen. I got back myself to instructing in June. The re-conversion had been a very leisurely affair. The OCU had shrunk in the last few years. There were, I think, only 6 QFIs. Rear crew instructor numbers had been reduced too. There was no doubt that squadron strength had reduced – hence the need to involve the OCU in operations – and replacements crews not forthcoming. And of course, there was this additional role the Vulcan had taken on; maritime reconnaissance. A dedicated course had been designed to accommodate training crews for that role. But it was less interesting. Even 27 Squadron aircraft had been painted with an extra protective coat of paint against salt corrosion. All low level was over the sea and there was a lot of high-level surveillance by the navigator radar. Indeed, he and his equipment were crucial to the job. OCU pilot training consisted chiefly of low-speed handling (circuits and rollers) some asymmetric work and practicing a few emergencies. There were very few first tourists on Vulcans, other than the odd co-pilots.

The OCU always had a USAF exchange aircrew as a member of staff. With one exception these were pilots chiefly with B52 experience. They did the course and it was always interesting to compare the work they had done before with flying the Vulcan. They were all in the rank of major. I can't think of one who did not enjoy his time on Vulcans. A few stories are worth relating without naming names.

When the OCU was at Finningley, the runway was close to the towns of Doncaster and Bawtry. The main road between the two towns was the A1 which was a straight road lit with sodium lamps at night and nearly parallel with the Finningley runway but some distance away. When the north eastern runway was in use, the left-hand visual circuits overflew just to the west of Bawtry. One of our USAF pilots doing visual circuits on his night conversion had got a little too far laterally from the runway on the downwind leg. As he turned left onto final approach, he lined up very nicely with the lit-up A1. His instructor let him settle on the approach then asked if he intended landing there. He then pointed out, some distance to the right, where the runway was. We all wondered how much more of the approach our major would have flown without recognising his error.

We also had a very large USAF exchange officer ex-B52 pilot, of Polish roots. When he put his hand on the control column, he enveloped nearly the whole thing which seemed to disappear from view. He was very pleasant and always had a joke during the pre-flight briefing in the planning room. One joke which stuck with me was the time he did the briefing and for the time check, he had put on a very large Mickey Mouse watch. "When Mickey's hand reaches the top of the dial…" Another time he said at the end of the briefing "If we crash and I survive and you die, can I have your watch?" Although he was a good pilot, he frightened me once when I was the duty instructor in the tower by starting his asymmetric overshoot well below the decision height of 200 feet above ground. There was not much free air below the aircraft when it reached sufficient speed to start climbing. The Vulcan came over the top of the air traffic tower at no more than 40 to 50 feet and very noisy too. It was no good diving under a desk for protection. We never did find out why he initiated the manoeuvre so late as the pilot accompanying him said they were already in a good position to land.

CHAPTER 28 - Characters

The OCU was not all work. We did have the odd bit of fun mainly at the expense of, sometimes senior officers, sometimes our visitors. Annually a reception was held for the local dignitaries. Mostly these were persons of repute, like the county's Lord Lieutenant, political leaders, pastors of local villages, etc.

At that particular reception the Chairman of West Lindsey District Council had been invited with his partner and a number of councillors. Jim W. was a first-class prankster. Jim's group decided that something should happen to the Chairman of the council, but what? Someone pointed out that this elevated politician had, round his neck, a chain of office, which would be a nice trophy for one of the squadrons. Chains of office are a series of badges and shields in precious metals joined by a chain of gold. They were quite valuable. Stealing one would be a big crime. That didn't stop Jim. He organised an electricity failure when all the guests were in the ante-room drinking sherry. It was dark outside and the room fell into darkness. There was a thump, an "ouch", followed by the lights coming back on a few seconds later. The leader's chain of office had disappeared. Some very deft fellow had removed it first by undoing the built-in safety pins tying the chain to the man's suit, lifted it over his head and disappeared without a trace. What a well organised robbery.

Following that, things did not go back to normal and the reception was abandoned. Eventually the chain found its way to one of the squadrons' offices and returned to West Lindsey. There was hell to pay but Jim W. owned to the prank and that was more or less it. I think that was the last time the council of West Lindsey was invited while the Vulcans were at Scampton.

By the time I re-joined the Vulcan QFI community, QFIs were not always allocated just one crew at a time to instruct. The standard was high from all the QFIs and it mattered little who flew with which crew. I managed to get a few instructional trips with one individual who I will never forget: Wilby C. Wilby was a graduate BA in modern languages from Queen's University, Belfast and an MA from Trinity College, Dublin. He had a very marked Belfast accent giving the impression that he was a thick Irishman. On the contrary he was one of the brightest persons I ever met. He used to say that if one wanted to overhear the best conversations, one took a bus either in Dublin or Paris. At the time I was doing a course with the Open University in geography and psychology. He read a couple of my essays in both subjects and judged the mark I would get for them very accurately. I don't think the RAF would ever be able to use all the intellectual talents he had.

There were quite a few stories about Wilby and his sharp and spontaneous wit. When he was a co-pilot his captain, a Squadron Leader named W., was a flight commander on a Scampton squadron. He was not well regarded, particularly by the ground crews. W. was the captain on one of the sorties which was short for an engine air test. Because the aircraft radar was not serviceable, the Navigator Radar was not required and left the aircraft to wait for transport in the servicing hut adjoining the dispersal. The captain started the engines and began taxying without the crew chief giving the all clear. The poor man was nearly run over. Back in the hut, the chief swore at the captain calling him foul names. After the flight, the crew met at the bar and the captain, feeling somewhat guilty of nearly killing the crew chief, asked the navigator what the chief had said. "I'd rather not say", replied the man. "Go on, tell me. What did he say?", "Well, Sir, he called you a F***ing turd". W. turned to Wilby and said "What do you think of that, Wilby?", who replied, "Sir, this is a very rude thing to say, but a fine example of an English understatement!". Another time W. called Wilby who was walking by his office and said, "Wilby I've just rearranged my office. What do you think?". "Sir", Wilby replied, "it's an improvement, you are standing where the rubbish bin used to be." At a cocktail party a girl being flirted with by Wilby, said referring to his thick Belfast accent: "At least I am articulate." "Yes", he said, "like a lorry." He was not a bad pilot either.

****

On RAF stations, daily an officer is nominated to be the Orderly Officer whose duty was to look after the place outside working hours. The OO slept in the officers' mess. On larger stations a more senior officer was nominated to be Senior Duty Officer. On these stations, the OO was always of Pilot Officer or Flying Officer rank, and the SDO a Flight Lieutenant. On V-Force stations there were plenty of Fg. Off. from the squadrons but others such as air traffic controllers, administrative officers, engineering officers were also eligible to be nominated. One of

172

the duties the OO had to carry out was to ensure that the Armoury was secure (in case of IRA attack?), and to perform a random security check on one aircraft on a dispersal pan. At Scampton, one of the dispersals was near the operations block. This young OO principal job was in administration. He decided to do his security check in the dark in the early evening, and rather than drive on the taxiway to a dispersal across the airfield, he took a short walk across the grass from the Operations Block towards the near-by dispersal Foxtrot, approaching it behind a parked Vulcan. What he did not know was that if the navigation and anti-collision light are on, the engines are either running or about to start. The lights were on and engines about to be started. In the aircraft, the first-pilot was all set up for a multiple rapid engine start. The throttles were set, the fuel was on and he pressed the rapid start button. All four engines started winding up but no jet pipe temperatures. He looked down at the start panel and noticed that he had neglected to switch the ignition on, which he promptly did. By then much fuel unburned had been fed to the engines' combustors. When the ignitors burst into life, the fuel lit up with a whoosh and four fireballs were ejected from jet pipes in the direction of the walking OO who, fortunately, was sufficiently far away to be unharmed but very, very frightened. The security check went undone.

CHAPTER 29 – Low Fuel

When the Vulcan Mk2 came into service, the minimum landing fuel was 8,000 lbs. This is 1,000 gallons (4,500 litres). This seems a lot but the fuel was spread quite thinly over the large number of fuel tanks in the wings. Eventually, for safety reasons, the minimum was increased to 10,000 lbs. Nevertheless, there was always the possibility of being forced to land well below the minimum. Such happened to me on the way to Goose Bay. We had been fighting headwinds (jet stream strength) nearly all the way. Although the forecast Goose Bay weather was acceptable, by the time we received their actual weather it was deteriorating below the forecast. We eventually attempted one approach but never saw the runway. So off we went to our alternate, Loring Air Force Base in Maine, some 500 miles away, the nearest airfield with suitable weather. We were not flush with fuel and the expected arrival fuel at Loring was well below the minimum.

The biggest fuel tanks in the Vulcan were numbers 1 and 2 on each side. They were just above the nosewheel bay and had the maximum effect on the control of the centre of gravity (CG) of the aircraft. The tanks were cube shaped rather than the large flat rubber bags in the wings. As the aircraft becomes lighter, weight of fuel in one tank has an increasing effect on the CG. Normally CG control was automatic but once the fuel was down to minimum CG control was done manually.

The time to Loring from the overshoot at Goose Bay was about one hour fifteen minutes. The aircraft was light, so the climb to cruising level would use only about 3,000 to 4,000 lbs of fuel and take 8 minutes. The high-level portion followed by the descent would be about 60 to 70 minutes. I very much hoped for straight-in approach to the runway at Loring. Altogether I reckoned we would need about 10,000 lbs of fuel. At our overshoot, we had just 13,000 lbs. Landing at Loring with just 3,000 lbs was somewhat worrying. I could have declared an emergency to give us priority to get that that straight-in approach, but that was last resort. The low fuel handling procedure had been worked out in the simulator but never used in anger. I hoped the procedure would work.

The low fuel handling drill was really quite simple. The system to control the CG is left running automatically until 8,000 lbs of fuel is reached then switched off. Fuel is transferred from numbers 7 and 1 tanks to get as much fuel as possible in numbers 1 and 2 tanks on both sides but still within CG limits. The pumps in those front tanks are turned off and fuel is used from the wing tanks always keep watch on the CG. The procedure worked very well. We landed with about 3,000 lbs of fuel. We refuelled and turned the aircraft round (checked the oil and top up some air cylinders) and off we went to Offutt AFB in Iowa, breathing more easily!

****

Often when flying in North America at our usual cruising levels above, mostly well above 40,000 feet, we would hear an airliner pilot ask the air traffic controller what type of aircraft was flying well above them. Airliners normally cruise between

31,000 and 39,000 feet with a few exceptions. Occasionally, for the hell of it and to show off, we would climb to 50,000 feet[22] and report our position on the same radio frequency as civilian traffic.   The position report would say that we were overhead Chicago, at Flight Level 500. That often would attract comments from those flying below us.

---

[22] This was much against the regulations because we were not wearing appropriate O2 clothing, inflatable jerkin and g-trousers, but on the other hand, throughout its life the Vulcan never suffered from an accidental cabin depressurisation.

CHAPTER 30 – Lone Ranger Lightning Strike and Whiskey

Lone or Western rangers did not come often to the OCU. Mainly because unlike squadron crews, we just flew to destinations and operational crews flew low level sorties in Canada and the US as well as engage in fighter affiliation at low as well as high level. On one occasion we were asked to fly to an Italian Air Force base at Istrana, not far from Venice on a Thursday then on Friday fly a low-level route along the west Italian coast, followed by flying to Akrotiri in Cyprus for the weekend, returning back to Scampton the following Monday.

The first part as far as Cyprus went well, but we had arrived at Istrana took late to take the train to Venice. That pleasure would have to wait. Parts of the Italian coast were spectacular particularly as the route started south of Sicily, round the island with Etna smoking away quietly, and as far north as Rome. But the weather in Cyprus that weekend was not good and some people in the crew cursed the Greek gods residing on Mount Olympus.

The aircraft behaved well and we took off on time on Monday. On the climb out we were struck by lightning (the only time this happened to me, and a lesson not to curse Greek gods). There was a loud crump, dust rose above the coaming below the windscreen and settled again; nothing else. We levelled off and did a thorough check of all systems, particularly the compasses which could have been badly affected. The AEO checked the external part of the aircraft with his periscope.

Everything was working so I decided to carry on home. There were airfields all the way home, into which we could dash if required. Back at Scampton the crew chief had a good look at the airframe and saw that the lightning bolt had entered the aircraft at the tip of the flight refuelling probe and left at the top of the tail. There were a few scorch marks there but no other damage. This was soon repaired.

One Ranger that was unusual was to Gardermoen, a Norwegian Air Force base some 20 miles from Oslo. One of the navigators knew that the price of alcohol in Norway was prohibitive so he decided, unknown to me, to engage in a bit of black market. He managed to get a case of good quality whiskey tax free in bond, delivered to the aircraft just before we climbed in. He said it was a gift for the Norwegian Air Force base commander. I did not enquire further.

There seemed to be no custom or immigration check at Gardermoen when we landed on the military side. We were met by a few Norwegian Air Force aircrew and once the bomb bay panier had been emptied and the Vulcan had been post-flight checked – air, oil and fuel – we left it for the weekend. Our black-market navigator made certain that a bottle of whiskey was quickly dispatched to the base commander, and via the aircrew that had met us, advertise the rest at a large profit. All was sold in a matter of minutes. Compared to the usual Norwegian price for a bottle of whisky, his bottles were cheap, very cheap. I subsequently found out that this black market was a common thing whenever UK based aircraft were on detachment in Norway.

The rest of the weekend was occupied visiting Oslo including a boat trip on the loch adjoining the city. It seemed a pleasant city but we did not consume much alcohol with beer at £5 a bottle. On the boat trip, there was an amusing American full of one liners and stories. We saw a largish yacht towing a small empty boat behind. The small boat was pitching and rolling badly in the bigger boats wake. Our American said this was the mother-in-law boat.

On Monday morning we took off on time, did an Astro navigation halfway across the Atlantic trip before returning to Scampton.

CHAPTER 31 – Number 1 Group Standardisation Unit

In mid-1978 I was posted to what I considered was the best job I could think of; as a standardiser (examiner) on Number 1 Group Standardisation Unit (GSU). The GSU staff consisted of two pilots, two navigators – a bomb aimer and a plotter - and an AEO, assisted by two typists and a clerk. Our job was to test, examine, and report on all aspects of flying the Vulcan as well as the aircrew side of administration of each squadron. This included reviewing the checklist, operating procedures, and various orders. Each operational squadron crewmember was examined in the air at least once during their tour of duty, and would be subjected to a ground oral examination at least once also. The flying and ground instructors of the OCU would also be tested, as were those in the flight simulator. Renewing of category and re-categorisation of QFIs was also done by the GSU. It was a job without equal. I remember once talking to a squadron commander who said jokingly "Now that you are on the GSU, we have to address you as 'Sir'".

I had to bring myself up to speed on all kinds of information as well as learn the ropes of an examiner. Although I was used to writing reports, the style and format the GSU had adopted over the years was unique. With time, the unit had grown into a bit of a monster in the eyes of Vulcan crews. GSU examiners were "trappers". The name says it all. Crews obviously respected the checking officers but fundamentally, they were in fear of them. The GSU checkers, on the other hand made themselves difficult to approach, and even more difficult to get straight answers from them. I had had experience of that myself on more than one occasion. I could never work out whether the person I asked did not know the answer or was too haughty to tell me (see foot-note above about auto-pilot disengagement).

The man in charge, Vic Ayres, and I decided that this had to change. Of course, GSU staff checked people's ability and standards and could make a difference to their future if they did not come up to scratch. Neither of us was of a mind to maintain the "keep your distance" policy. One of our predecessors was so uncommunicative and straight faced that someone once joked, "Somebody must have died. I have just seen J.A. smile". We started by writing to all the squadrons advising them of our Open-Door Policy. We were available to answer reasonable questions, or interpretations of procedures or rules. That alone had a considerable effect. People started to smile and nod at us. We visited squadron crew rooms for a cup of coffee and a general chat. Suddenly we were accepted as part of the Vulcan force and not as a unit that stood above it. It made a great difference to the results of our check rides. Our demanding standards did not drop but because crews being checked were less tense, they tended to perform better. Those who did not come up to standard were debriefed thoroughly and their supervising officers advised. Only on one occasion did I recommend a captain, who was also the squadron QFI, to be suspended. I found that painful and upsetting.

Each member of the GSU controlled the work he did. Check flights were arranged well in advance. Although we were based at Scampton, we belonged to No.1 Group. No one checked whether we were at work or not, unlike all the previous units I had worked on. Station exercises did not affect us and we took no direct part in the running of any of it. At least not at the beginning of my tour. After a few months, I felt I was well on top of the job. If there was no flying to be done, or reports to write, I would go home. I suppose that I had reached to top of my professional tree when I was posted to the GSU. We were agents of Central Flying School, which was "the standard" for pilots not only in the RAF but also in many Commonwealth countries. Recall that the RCAF instructional course I did in Canada was identical to the RAF's Central Flying School's and was monitored by RAF CFS agents. Part of the introduction to the new job was an interview by the Commandant of CFS. It was all very relaxed but I noticed the Air Commodore was limping and had a large dressing on his foot. It turned out that his big toe had been cut off by his Flymo mower and that without big toe, he found balancing difficult. I resolved to get rid of our Flymo without delay.

Flying for the GSU meant that we could authorise all flights. That is, we did not have to rely on any superior officer for authority to fly. This was a considerable privilege, which I had not appreciated until then. The two pilots of the GSU were literally free agents with full autonomy. On flights abroad, the USA, Canada, Italy, Cyprus, we went when we wanted, no questions asked. We were our own bosses with little supervision but exercising such professionalism, that no one ever questioned any aspects of our work.

****

Dick F., who had been my last co-pilot at the end of my tour on 617 squadron in 1968 had been posted to Canberras. I next heard of him from a friend who was in charge of RAF Sports Parachuting at an airfield near Brize Norton. The club flew Britten Norman Islanders and Dick was their pilot. By that time, he had been a flight lieutenant for some time and wanted to get on. He decided to write to the Air Vice Marshal, Air Member for Personnel. He wrote that among those he saw on promotion lists, he always recognised one person who he knew was an idiot. Could he please be that idiot in the next list? Dick did not get an answer, nor promotion although I expect there were lots of belly laughs in Whitehall. Instead, he got posted back to Vulcans as a co-pilot, picking up where he left off some 8 years previously.

In due course Dick started his Intermediate Co-pilot Course and I was asked to carry out his Final Handling Test which included a captaincy potential assessment. Dick handled the crew and the aircraft most competently. I was more than satisfied with his performance when I gave him a simulated emergency resulting in a practice diversion to Leeming, in Yorkshire. After the overshoot, he rightly decided to return to Scampton at 2,500 feet, or so, air traffic safety being provided by airfield radars on the way back. Out of Leeming's surveillance we were handed to Linton-on-Ouse radar. Dick recognised the air traffic controller's voice and, rather than stick to normal radio telephony (R/T) discipline, proceeded to have what I could only describe as a telephone conversation with the controller. I was surprised by this action. At Scampton, we did a few circuits and landed.

The trip debrief took place as usual facing each other both with a relaxing coffee. I asked Dick why he had had this chat with the Linton controller. His response was that he thought that his final handling test had finished once the practice diversion was completed. I said that very sadly, (this was to me a personal emotion) I could not recommend him for captaincy. Although he was older by at least 8 years since we flew together on 617 Squadron, he had not matured and this breach of R/T discipline told me such. I was truly disappointed.

CHAPTER 32 - Diversity

Some trips were interesting. The USAF had an agreement with the RAF in allowing bomber crews to fly continental US low-level routes. The provisos were that the GSU would sample the route first, and then brief Vulcan crews prior to their departure from the UK. The USAF changed its routes frequently and although there was a wide choice, we selected those routes trying to duplicate the sort of terrain crews would traverse in wartime. We operated from Offutt US Air Force base near Omaha, Nebraska. New routes would come up every four months or so. We went to Offutt at the same frequency. Omaha was a typical mid-western American town with nothing attractive in particular, or unattractive for that matter. On one of our trips, there was a classical music concert in the combined concert hall and museum. These concerts generally took place at "Brunch time" on Sundays. They were well attended. I went a couple of times and quite pleased to have done so. One Sunday morning I cycled from Offutt to the museum, a distance of about 10 miles, and no traffic. It was so unusual for anyone to arrive on a bike, (a bit sweaty too) that I was singled out by the Master of Ceremonies for my dedication to good music.

We did other trips to the US. We organised a visit to our counterparts in Strategic Air Command. Their tasks were to assess B52 crews. They were based, I seem to remember at Offutt AFB, the home of Strategic Air Command.

The system used by SAC was fundamentally different from ours. They had what amounted to a tick list which was labelled Satisfactory or Unsatisfactory. If any of the dozens of items was ticked unsatisfactory, the crew was deemed to have failed the check ride. The checking officer occupied the jump seat between the two pilots and had no part in the running of the flight other than, at specific points, call a simulated emergency. The report consisted of the form on which the tasks had been ticked.

We operated a system which was based on written reports of between 300 and 400 words. Although we had a short tick list, the labels were "Commendable; Very Satisfactory; Satisfactory: and Unsatisfactory. The narrative expanded on the tick list. On the whole it was the written report which held more authority. We were told that both the Senior Air Staff Officer, normally an Air Commodore, and the Air Officer Commanding Number 1 Group always read our crew reports. We thought we had a better more comprehensive system although it took much more time to prepare.

The Unit's annual squadron visits lasted 5 days. It was meant to examine records including logbooks (it was odd how we seem to find the ones which contained errors. We were always assured that all the rest were correct). It was also an opportunity to subject crews to oral tests and for the lucky few, flight simulator rides. It was unusual, perhaps even rare that squadrons were not up to a good standard. I can't remember ever visiting one such. At the end of the week, we debriefed the squadron executives, the OC, flight commanders and branch leaders (pilots, navigators and AEOs). The OC GSU would read out his overall findings and each specialist would go through his week's work. One of us, George always introduced an unusual word in his report which we had much fun discovering and smile as we did. The others wondered why the mirth. Much later in a BA flight to Atlanta to see my sister, the co-pilot was an ex-Vulcan man. He took me on the flight deck of the Tristar and told the story of the time he and his captain were examined. The result I gave, he said, was "satisfactory". But, he added, since he had answered all my questions, why the result was not "commendable". Apparently, I replied that I had not asked any commendable questions!

****

Annually, the RAF was invited to take part in the USAF Strategic Air Command Bombing Competition. Strike Command had won the competition a few times. The rules were changed to include low-level fighter interception. The fighter squadron taking part was based in northern Florida, near Panama City. Their pilots were not familiar with the Vulcan and wanted to do some intercepts to judge the aircraft's capability as well as the way it would look on their radars. On the way to northern Florida, as we were flying to the west of Washington D.C., the air traffic controller asked if we could see the ground where we were. "We can indeed. It's all clear". "OK" he said, "I've never seen your type of aircraft before and you're about to overfly us. I'll just pop out to have a look at you". "Fine", we replied, "You should be able to pick us out, and we are con-trailing". A few minutes later, he came back on line and said, "I saw you clearly. You guys sure look pretty up there". Out of devilment I said, "Are you a tall guy with a moustache?", "Yes I am". "Well, we saw you too", and left it at that. I still wonder if that man ever believed that the RAF had such wonderful kit as to be able to distinguish a tall man with a moustache from 40,000feet.

In Florida, we planned a single sortie of about 2 hours at about 400 feet above ground and 320 knots over the wooded terrain surrounding the air base. The idea was that we should demonstrate evasive manoeuvres that crews could take during interceptions. When the fighters were closing in on us, we would slow we would slow down to below 200 knots. At that speed, with up to 60 degrees of bank (within the g limits) we easily out turned the F106, Delta Dart. The USAF had not considered this. It was eventually recommended that RAF crews would reduce their speed to no less than about 250 knots and not use over 45 degrees of bank. This at least gave fighter aircraft enough speed to stay in the air albeit with limited manoeuvrability. As it turned out, once again the RAF won the competition that year with no valid fighter interceptions. The 250 knots and 45 degrees of bank limits were not really observed or heard of.

We also tested Italian low-level routes. We flew into and from Istrana in Northern Italy, near the town of Treviso. We were accommodated in the Carlton or the Ritz Hotels in Treviso, both being 4-star standard. There was a good train service from there to Venice every 30 minutes. It is only some 30 kilometres away. The first time we went was in February. We arrived mid-afternoon and after putting the aircraft to bed, we used an Italian Air Force crew coach to take us to our hotel. As soon as we had cleaned up, we took the train to Venice. We arrived at

Santa Lucia station at dusk. The station gives directly onto the Grand Canal. For me that was one of the most emotional experience of my life. To see Venice, the Grand Canal at that time of day was a scene without compare. Public lighting was coming on setting these wonderful buildings and bridges in a glow that I find no word to describe. I cried for the sheer beauty of it. Even now as I think of that end of day, I am moved.

The trip to Italy ended with a flight to Cyprus for the weekend. We were back at Scampton on Monday. On one occasion, in November, the weather forecast for Istrana was reasonable but as we overflew Milan, we were told that Istrana weather was thick fog, as were all the airfields south of the Alps. Our alternate airfield was back at Scampton since we had plenty of fuel. However, we were told, Aviano was wide open. We had no idea where Aviano was or the type of airfield it was. We soon found out its details from the various aeronautical information manuals we had, and 30 minutes later, we landed there. It turned out to be a CIA airfield used by the USAF on occasions. After wrapping up our aircraft for the night, we got a USAF bus to the local town. On the way there, I noticed a road sign pointing to Pian Cavallo, 15 kilometres. During that very week, my daughter was skiing at Pian Cavallo. We flew back to Istrana the following morning, the weather having cleared.

CHAPTER 33 – QRA Again?

A new boss took over the GSU, Ian Prior. I had had little to do with him other than checking him once previously. He turned out, like his predecessor to be a thoroughly likeable and professional man. We hit it off right away. I had to check him out so that he became a Command instrument-rating examiner. He took to the job like a duck to water. He was very interested in home computing. He bought a very early machine, which allowed him to do some programming. He got quite good at it. At the end of his tour, he went on a computer course at the joint Army/RAF school.

The Vulcan force declared to SACEUR (Supreme Allied Commander Europe) was running short of crews. Aircraft were being disposed of and squadrons were always short of crews. Number 27 Squadron having its role changed from bombing to maritime, reduced further the availability of combat ready crews. The GSU like the OCU before, had never taken part in exercises of any sort. But our time had come to participate. Number 1 Group Senior Air Staff Officer explained the situation to us and, hey presto, we were now a crew declarable to SACEUR. This was certainly a surprise not only to us but all these aircrew on the squadron always envious of our non-participation. But we took it like men and started to do some serious target studies, something we had not done is many years.

This was in 1979 and Jimmy Carter, a Democrat with very liberal views was president of the USA. For reasons I could never fathom out, he issued a directive which changed fundamentally NATO nuclear targeting. Up to that point targets were always military and as military people ourselves, we could understand the philosophy and accepted it, nasty as nuclear weapons are. Carter allowed populated areas, large towns and cities to become targets. There was always somewhat of a thin military side to them but we were going to bomb cities, if we ever got through. I remember clearly our target. It was a KGB Headquarters in the middle of Minsk. I remember also the satellite photos of our target. It was at the intersection of two major roads lined with buildings. When the picture was taken, vehicles were clearly visible. All of us were upset and bewildered that such targets were chosen with the implied agreement of the president of the US. Although we remarked adversely on this change of philosophy, we had no choice.

We took part in one or two Tactical Evaluation exercises (Taceval) which turned out to be very interesting and at times amusing. Between the various states of readiness to which we were brought up, we had to play games such as pretending we were in a trench, dodging an attack by a couple of Buccaneers. The trenches were plastic tape stuck on the grass, inside which many crews were meant to shelter. But it started raining so we moved the trench under a tree. We could not leave camp or even get back to our offices. We slept in camp beds in an office on the side of a hangar. The team running the Taceval even had a few of us pretend to be wounded to see how the others would deal with the problems. They didn't and we died. The actual flights were interesting too. It was high level to a descent point to begin our low level over Germany and, I think, going into the Netherlands. These were routes none of us had ever done and we enjoyed the novelty. I can't remember our bombing score but it must have been acceptable. In any case, because we were all standardisers, no one dared tell us if our results were rubbish.

****

I was once phoned by a squadron commander, asking me to do a check on his squadron QFI, Pete B. He felt the man was not up to scratch particularly with his circuit work. His previous job was flying instructor on JPs. He was a very experienced instructor but fairly new to Vulcans. I duly arranged a flight. I played the part of a new co-pilot who had shown problems with handling the aircraft mainly in the circuits. The flight was meant to be short and after a little upper air handling we returned to the circuit. It became obvious that Pete had not mastered the Vulcan in the circuit, specifically on final approach during an instrument or visual circuit. I had to take over twice during his demonstrations because if I had not, we could have hit the ground in the undershoot. I arranged the debriefing to be in front of the squadron commander as this was a very serious matter, which would affect his career. Pete was posted back to flying JPs, which in fact he much preferred. I must add that I had flown with him on a jet refresher course on JPs in Leeming a number of years previously, and remembered how impressed I was by his instructional skills.

As a checking officer, I examined some superb pilots and instructors together with their crew. One such was Neil

McDougall who was the 27 Squadron QFI. Number 27 Squadron was the only Vulcan unit whose role was maritime reconnaissance. I played the part of an experienced Vulcan captain just posted to the squadron. As a newcomer, I had to be shown the ropes. Let me tell you the story:

Neil briefed me fully before take-off. The standard sortie profile was to establish a large racetrack pattern at some 40,000 feet some distance north of Scotland. The Navigator Radar, using a modified H2S bombing radar, would be in charge of watching for unusual maritime activity in parts of the eastern Atlantic and the North Sea. Having reached our holding area, after some 40 minutes, the navigator said that there was a largish formation of ships in the North Sea, some 150 nautical miles off the Scottish coast, sailing southwest. In normal circumstances, a radio call would be made to the appropriate authority, which in turn would despatch a fighter or a Nimrod aircraft to investigate. But if the target was too far from land or no Nimrod was available, it was left to the aircraft captain to investigate the contact. The Vulcan was also equipped with a receiver that converted radar signals sweeping the aircraft into audible signals. These signals were all different and a skilled operator could distinguish the various types of radars illuminating the aircraft. These signals were available to the whole crew on the aircraft intercom system. Few pilots were experts in recognising these noises and left the analysis to the Air Electronics Officer. Although I knew a few radar audio signatures, I left the recommendation to the AEO. In this case, he advised the captain that the aircraft was being swept by a

Soviet radar normally fitted to large warships, such as the aircraft carrier Kiev.

Neil said that in a case like this, particularly that this was some considerable distance from fighter bases and no Nimrod available, we would investigate the radar return ourselves. This entailed descending to 500 feet over the sea, and approaching the target to no closer than 2 miles and not below 1,500 feet. As we got closer, the radar noise changed to a more insistent tone, indicating that we had been recognised and we being looked at more intensely. Some 10 miles from the target, the noise changed to a continuous tone indicating that the ship's defence radar was locked on us. This type of radar is associated with surface to air missiles. I wondered if we were being a bit too brave. The visibility was no more than 3 miles and I must admit that I was getting concerned about the safety of this exercise. Missiles could be launched at us at any instant. I said so to Neil who replied that we must do our best to take photos of the ship. By that time, I was more than concerned. Suddenly, at a distance of some 3 miles, a ship duly appeared out of the gloom directly ahead of us. It was a very large bulk carrier sailing serenely. I had been well and truly fooled. What Neal had done was to get the AEO to use a tape recorder with all the various Soviet radar noises feeding into the intercom. At the end of that exercise, I thought I had had a very good introduction to the maritime reconnaissance role. I gave Neal full marks.

Some years later, Neal was involved in the Falklands dispute flying the last Blackbuck attack on Stanley airfield. He ended up in Rio de Janeiro, having broken his flight-refuelling probe on the last refuelling top-up back to Ascension Island, his operating base. But that is another story.

Another time I was asked to investigate what was described as haunted Vulcans. Apparently, during flight, occasionally the control column moved from side to side of its own accord for no obvious reason. This movement lasted just a few seconds but when it happened, the captain rightly elected to return to base and land. This happened a few times to only one crew but on different Vulcans. I must explain that all the control runs, in the form of one-inch diameter tubes passed along the edge of the cabin by the navigator radar's position. Therefore, the navigator radar was suspected of somehow interfering with the run, perhaps using his feet. He had not been told that he was under suspicion.

On the flight, we carried out all the internal and external checks on the controls. All appeared normal. After take-off, passing about 20,000 feet the control column suddenly moved from side to side of its own accord. I decided to return to base and land. After landing, I ensured that I was left alone in the cabin to allow me to examine closely the control runs, to see if there were any witness marks. The runs were clear and the little dust on all the tubes completely undisturbed. I asked the crew chief to confirm what I had seen. My report to the squadron commander said that we did have a spurious control movement that I could not explain, and neither could I understand how it was done. In the event, the navigator was posted off the Vulcan force. This sort of thing never happened again. I was certain that the man interfered with the controls but remain intrigued as to how he did it.

****

In the GSU we had sometimes odd requests and deep questions most of which we could answer. Perhaps the most difficult ones were about interpretations of flying rules and regulations. Over the years Number 1 Group was renowned for tight control of its stations, squadrons and crews. The was not much freedom to do as one pleased. Once, during the course of an exercise, this blew up in the face of 1 Group. Crews had been brought up to readiness 02 which entailed aircraft starting engines and taxying to the runway holding point. Dependent on the whim of the Bomber Controller, crews could be released back to Readiness 15 or held there until they ran out of fuel. To relax the readiness state a code word was issued. On that particular occasion, the wrong code word was used and although most crews returned to their dispersal one captain insisted for the correct code word. It took a very long time to find. In spite of pleading by the Station Commander on external intercom, the captain would not budge until the correct code word was used. We were asked subsequently about that and whether that captain had done the right thing. This was way outside our terms of reference and we referred the questioner to 1 Group. However, we felt that that captain had adopted the correct stance although he made life very difficult for a few people. But he also provided some good laughs.

****

Once I was phoned by a flight commander of, I think, 50

Squadron at Waddington, Monty M. who said that one of the less experienced captains had a bit of a fright with XM599 doing visual circuits when he got himself cross controlled on the finals turn. So, Monty and the squadron QFI, Dave T. decided to fly the suspicious bomber. Brian B. was not kidding. XM599 flew like a corkscrew with a suicidal tendency to hit the ground on the finals turn below 150 knots. Dave, whom I knew from experience, was a very accurate pilot was quietly struggling. Both pilots came to the conclusion that the aircraft was bent and the rigging must be checked before someone got hurt in it. Everything was indeed checked and re-checked including re-setting elevons, weighing the aircraft and accurately measuring the CofG. After some months in the hangar, Monty asked me to accompany him for a short circuit detail to see how well repaired XM599 flew. This was months later of course. On March 16 1981, Monty M. and I climbed aboard and flew just 55 minutes during which we carried out 8 circuits. My comment to Monty at the end of the flight was: "Scrap it." XM599 never flew on that squadron again. This was a very rare event which I don't think had ever happened before or since. No doubt some Vulcans flew better than others. Some used more fuel or did not like it much above certain high speeds but never one like 599.

At Scampton, in the 1960s and 70s there was one aircraft, XL444 which was troublesome. The problems were mainly for the engineers and the aircraft spent long periods in the hangar being repaired. The engineers were tearing their hair out as when one fault was rectified and the aircraft flew it came back with a fault that could not be explained and difficult to correct. The Vulcan is an intricate piece of machinery. The surprising thing is that it flew at all. Yet there were sorties when we came back without a single unserviceability. To be fair, I would estimate that perhaps 30% to 50% of our trips were cancelled due to system unserviceability. It was something we had to live with, frustrating as it was at times. But XL444 was special (the name Treble 4 was modified to Trouble 4). The engineers gave it a formal title of "rogue aircraft". Unlike the average product made of many bits, manufacturing tolerances tend to cancel each other out. In 444 they added to each other. I had a car like that once. It was generally termed a Friday afternoon car. I don't suppose there could be such a thing as a Friday afternoon Vulcan, but the label fitted well.

CHAPTER 34 – More of Various

Although I loved my job, I had become somewhat dissatisfied with the RAF way of doing certain things. I was specialist aircrew and expected to get promotion to Squadron Leader. My appraisals were all excellent with strong recommendation for promotion. Specialist aircrew Squadron Leader was the maximum rank I could reach and I felt I deserved it. My service record in Cyprus, the OCU and now the GSU all proved I was worthy of it. However, there was no sign of promotion so I applied for premature voluntary retirement (PVR) in late 1979. The RAF had made many people redundant in the mid-70s, and like all such large organisation had overdone the redundancy.[23] They were now running short of aircrew. My application for PVR was accepted but with a date of late December 1982, three years on. Previously, the normal delay before being released was 6 months. I contacted the Civil Aviation Authority (CAA) to obtain advice on getting civilian licences. All I had to do was to take the ground examinations and fly a light twin aircraft for an instrument-rating test. This was not difficult and I started looking round for likely civilian schools that could provide me with this service. There was such a school at Humberside airport. That was ideal. I also started to put a few feelers out for likely employment. Near Lincoln, there

---

[23] The winning crew from a USAF SAC Bombing and Navigation competition returned to RAF Waddington to be greeted by the station and squadron commanders, together with crew families. After greeting his wife and children, the captain of the crew was handed a blue envelope by his wife. It was obviously an official envelope from the MOD containing perhaps a congratulatory message, maybe even a medal. It was his redundancy notice!

was as small airport, Wickenby, run by two brothers. They had a couple of Embraer light twin aircraft able to carry seven or eight passengers. I wanted to get back to air taxi as I had done on the C45 Expeditor in the RCAF. Things were starting to fall into place.

Vulcan squadrons had started to be disbanded before the Falklands dispute, and many aircraft had been disposed of (I hope XM599 and XL444 among them). Some were sold to individuals, some for scrap, and some flown to various destinations including museums in the UK, Canada and the USA. One Vulcan ended as "gate guard" at RAF Waddington where all versions of the aircraft, Marks 1, 1A and 2, had served since 1956.

One Vulcan went to RAF Catterick in North Yorkshire, at the time the RAF Fire Fighting School. The runway at Catterick is short, only 3,000 feet long (under 900 metres), and the western end of the runway abuts on the very busy Great North Road, the A1. As GSU pilots, we were tasked to deliver an aircraft to Catterick. We flew over just to check the approach and get a feeling for the place. Once there, the Vulcan was to be used as a fire trainer. Not a nice end for such a fine warrior. The only equipment left in the aircraft was sufficient to allow us to fly it there. All the radar, ECM, navigation equipment had been taken out. Fuel loading was minimal too.

Due to the proximity to the very busy, dual carriageway A1, it was decided to close that road for the time we were expected to land. The Vulcan had prodigious brakes. Those

200

combined with the low weight and slow approach and landing speed and streaming of the brake parachute as soon as the wheels touched the ground at the very beginning of the runway, we stopped in about 1,500 feet. At the end of the runway, we could see all the TV and radio paraphernalia people waiting for us (perhaps expecting us to hang our flight refuelling probe over the A1 or even crash onto it). Both of us in the front looked at each other and although we discussed taxiing to the end of the runway to make a grand entrance/exit, we stopped where we were and waited for the press to come to us. It was quite amusing to see the paparazzi running down to meet us. A 1,500 feet walk is a long way carrying heavy TV kit.

After landing at RAF Catterick. The Vulcan dominating the background

RAF Catterick, the GSU crew, after landing

****

Sometime later, I was tasked by No 1 Group to find out if the runway at Winthorpe, a WW2 bomber airfield near Newark, was suitable for a Vulcan to land. The Newark Air Museum had been chosen to display a Vulcan owned by a Lincolnshire trust, to add to its expanding collection. I left Scampton on a misty, foggy day when I knew there would be little flying. Once I had found the airfield, which was not easy, I measured the length of the potential runway using the car odometer. It was about 4,000 feet long, but needed sweeping as it was strewn with small stones. I was about to depart when the fog lifted somewhat, and I saw some very large electricity pylons a short distance to the east of the runway running at 90 degrees to it. In my report to No 1 Group, I stipulated that the landing needed to take place when there was a fairly strong easterly wind. As it turned out, the aircraft landed in February 1983 between snow showers. This was hardly surprising, as in the east of England, at that time of year, an easterly wind will nearly invariably carry snow or sleet showers.

****

In February 1982, my old student Air Marshal David Craig who was Commander-in- Chief-designate of Strike Command asked me to arrange a farewell flight to salute the end of 35 Squadron of which he had been the officer commanding in the 1960s. I managed to get an OCU crew together with a Scampton aircraft. At Cottesmore, where Tornadoes were based, the weather prevented them from getting airborne to formate on us, but we managed to get an approach and a roller. The CinC had a quiet smile on his face that these wonderfully modern aircraft were beaten by the weather but we were not by our old chunk of machinery. While airborne, we managed also to do some low level and a fair amount of circuit work. Amazingly, the Scampton circuit was entirely free of other traffic unlike the usual crowding. I wondered why?

Air Marshal Sir David Craig's flight to salute the end of 35 Squadron

****

In 1982, a certain General in Argentina, following his interpretation of an implied invitation by the British government, invaded South Georgia, then the Falklands. The UK government had withdrawn the surveillance ship, HMS Endurance, and it was obvious that there was little to oppose Galtieri and his junta. The government decided to take on the Argentinians and started organising a retake of the islands.

It was decided to use Vulcans to bomb the runway at Stanley, the capital of the Falklands so as to stop the Argentinian Air Force from using that runway for its Mirage and A4B Sky Hawks missile launchers and fighter bombers. Although the Vulcan had been designed for air-to-air refuelling, it took a huge effort by the RAF to make a number of Vulcans up to flight refuelling standards. The system had been neglected. Although the Mk 1 model had used air-to-air refuelling for the non-stop flight of three Vulcans to Australia, the Mk 2 systems were never used. It took a lot of effort to get them going. In addition, the aircraft were modified to carry wing-mounted rockets. Inertial navigation systems no longer being used in other aircraft types, were quickly installed. The flight from Ascension to Stanley was well over 3,000 miles over the ocean and accurate navigation was required. Celestial navigation was useful but not sufficiently accurate.

What surprised me was that major modifications were carried out on the Vulcans and tested in a matter of days. There seemed to be no limit to the costs. Everyone worked their fingers to the bone to get the aircraft ready. This contrasted with requests for modifications that had been made in peacetime for which mostly the answer was no! If a modification was agreed, it would take a long time, sometime years to implement unless it had to do with flight safety. The British armed forces won the battle of the Falklands in June 82. However, there was a lot of luck in it. The effort to bomb the runway although admirable did not produce particularly good results.[24]

---

[24] I must add that many years later at the Newark Air Museum, I talked to a retired soldier who had taken part in the battle and subsequently stayed in Stanley. He said that the Stanley runway was built on a bog. Steel plates were used over the soft ground, over which re-enforced concrete was poured. The bomb burst through to the bog. It took much work and filling by the Royal Engineers to bring to runway up to serviceability.

CHAPTER 35 – Cheating?

After the debrief following a crew flight test, we were chatting when the captain said that they had just come back from Offutt, having done a couple of US Air Force low level routes. He was surprised and upset that the allowances paid to crews on Rangers had been cut by a substantial amount. I was rather intrigued by that, as I knew that rates were set in Queen's Regulations (QR), of course as amended from time to time. Apparently, there had been no QR amendment but the rates had changed. I talked to the station accountant who confirmed that the new rates had been published by HQ Strike Command.

I started investigating why the change had taken place in spite of QRs' clear statements what the rates were. I phoned first Strike Command who confirmed the changes. I pointed out the relevant QR but it made no difference. The rates were set, not according to QRs, and station accounts were instructed to use them. I found that increasingly intriguing, and decided to find out how and by whom QRs are written and kept up to date. Eventually I found that each regulation is sponsored by a department of the RAF (sometimes in conjunction with the other services). Specifically, I wanted to know who sponsored the regulation relevant to allowances when on temporary duty abroad, as in this case. I phoned the relevant department asking if amendments to the rates were about to be issued. None was. I then pointed out that Strike Command was in breach of the regulation. I was thanked for this information. I left it at that and waited to see results, if any.

Results were soon obvious, but not quite what I expected. Since this was the end of the Vulcan operational life, the Unit had been taken over by an old friend, Ken Pilbeam. Within a day of my call to the regulation's sponsor at the Ministry of Defence, Ken came in to the office with a face like thunder. "John, I want to talk to you. I've just saved you from a fate worse than death!", "What's all this", I said. He then related to me that he had a stormy meeting with the Station Commander about my meddling in affairs that did not regard me. I thought they did regard me and us too. We would be affected by the change in allowances should we go on temporary duty abroad. However, that is not the way the RAF functions. The first reaction in Strike Command was to attack the person who found them out, the prospective whistle blower, rather than try to get the regulation's sponsor to amend it, or pay the correct rates. I let the matter go since I was leaving the service in a matter of months. I pointed out to Ken that he should have been supporting me rather than accept the reactions of Strike Command. What it boiled down to was that Strike Command needed to save money and they tried to achieve this in an underhand and illegal way. In the last few years of my service, in my view, RAF management deteriorated. The example of my having to wait three years to be released, when a year prior to my request, the maximum wait time was six months, shows how things had become.

CHAPTER 36 - Illness

In June '82, I started to get some rather strange noises in my ears. It was like an echo and occasionally I would get a bout of vertigo. I took medical advice and I was tested to establish what the problem was. I even went to the Institute of Aviation Medicine in Farnborough where some extensive tests were carried out. The diagnosis was that I was now suffering from Menière syndrome. I had lost some 65% of my hearing in my right ear and I heard a loud constant noise (tinnitus) on that side.

My last Vulcan flight was a standardisation check on a co-pilot in XL427 on June 17th 1982. Soon after, I lost my flying category and although I was offered a ground job, I decided to leave the service. The RAF was quite generous. An old mate of mine was looking after my personnel file, my "desk officer". He suggested that I withdraw my PVR, which would allow me to be invalided out of the service. The advantages were considerable. My pension would be increased by some 12%, it would be index-linked from the date of my retirement, rather than have to wait until I became 55. My lump sum would reflect the increase in my pension, and if I wanted to commute any of the pension, it would be on terms that are more favourable.

Although I left the RAF officially on 24th December 1982, with accumulated leave from various schemes, (disability, terminal and Domcol [25]) I left Scampton in August. The Vulcan soon followed and was finally retired from the RAF just two

---

[25] Having joined the RAF from Canada, I was entitled to accumulate, I think, 5 days of unused leave every year for a maximum of five years.

years later. I received a number of cards, some from on high, saying how sorry they were that I had lost my medical category and decided to leave. I was sorry to leave too. It had been a very good part of my life, lasting over 20 years. It had ups and downs but many more ups than downs. For that I am grateful to all those with whom I worked and played too. I've had a grand time.[26]

---

[26] In 1990, a friend who was an ENT specialist and I were talking about my Meniere's disease. He asked how many bouts of dizziness had I had since I was diagnosed. "None" I replied. "I'll arrange for another diagnosis from a very good ENT man in Cambridge. Although it will cost, you might be able to go back to flying". I paid, and with much better diagnostic tools, it was concluded that in 1982, I had had a viral attack. I regained my flying licence but stayed in Information Technology. I just flew minis-with-wings: Cessna 152.

POSTSCRIPT

I retired and moved to France with Carole in 1999 and lived there for 20 years. That was the period when the Vulcan to the Sky trust managed to get XH558 in the air. I was sorry that I was too far away to be involved. I certainly would have volunteered my services. Who knows, they might even be accepted. Now I can just dream of flying the Vulcan again. I do, frequently.

When I returned to the UK in 1999, I joined the Newark Air Museum as a volunteer "Cockpit Opener". The static Vulcan is XM594, landed there by Neil McDougall (the man who gave me such a fright approaching what I thought was the Kiev, and who landed in Rio on his way back from the Falklands).

I've enjoyed initially displaying the Vulcan cabin to groups of 4 or 5. Covid-19 took over for a while and we ran a 30 minutes talk about the exterior of the Vulcan, interspersed with cold war stories here and there. The money raised from these events is used to keep control of corrosion on all the aircraft parked outside in all-weathers an endless job. I enjoy this type of hobby; it is good fun.

When I consider that XM594 has been sitting there for nearly 40 years, it still remains in acceptable condition. But like me, it is feeling its age. It is an endless task to keep beautiful (the Vulcan, not me). And that is what the Vulcan was: beautiful; threatening and aggressive looking, but with such elegance and grace of movement. I wrote above about the high regard the Lancaster continues to be held in the mind of the

British. It should be the same for all the V-Bombers. At the International Bomber Command Centre near Lincoln, no Vulcan nor Victor, nor Valiant is mentioned. Yet these aircraft were 'Bomber Command' for a long time, but their names are neglected.

Although I don't want to live in the past, I find as I grow older that I like to relive the many wonderful memories of my 20 years flying Vulcans. They come flooding back and I can't reduce my enthusiasm for the aircraft.

Lincoln, 2021

Printed in Great Britain
by Amazon